A DIALOGUE OF
CIVILIZATIONS

A DIALOGUE OF CIVILIZATIONS

Gülen's Islamic Ideals and Humanistic Discourse

B. Jill Carroll

Published by The Light, Inc.
26 Worlds Fair Dr. Unit C
Somerset, New Jersey, 08873, USA

www.thelightpublishing.com

Library of Congress Cataloging-in-Publication Data

Carroll, B. Jill, 1963-
A dialogue of civilizations : Gulen's Islamic ideals and humanistic discourse / B. Jill Carroll.
        p. cm.
Includes bibliographical references and index.
ISBN 978-1-59784-110-8
1. Gülen, Fethullah--Views on Islam. 2. Islam and humanism. 3. Islam--20th century. I. Title.
BP190.5.H78C37 2007
297.092--dc22

                                2007000765

Printed by
Victor Graphics, Baltimore, Maryland.

CONTENTS

FOREWORD

The twenty-first century has become a period of unheralded crisis. There are those who are devoted to violence, death, and destruction and, thankfully, there are those who challenge these ideas by championing the benefits of dialogue and understanding. The events of September 11, 2001 illustrate the importance of this. Events that day and the ongoing War on Terror have changed the landscape of both our local and international communities. In so doing, the nineteen hijackers created one of the greatest paradoxes of the twenty-first century: Islam, which sees itself as a religion of peace, is now associated with murder and mayhem.

There is an unfortunate lack of knowledge about Islam among both Muslims and non-Muslims alike. The need to understand Islam now reaches beyond the humanities departments of our universities and into the home of every individual. The ever-growing Muslim population is now estimated at 1.4 billion living in fifty-seven Muslim states, at least one of which has nuclear capabilities. Many of these Muslim states play a pivotal role either as close ally or adversary of the United States in the War on Terror. The Muslim community is not isolated to one part of the world; roughly seven million Muslims live in the United States and many millions more in Europe. The main terrorists on America's wanted list are Muslim—Osama bin Laden, Al Qaeda, and Taliban leaders such as Mullah Omar—but so are America's main allies in the War on Terror, President Pervez Musharraf of Pakistan, President Karzai of Afghanistan, and King Abdullah of Jordan. Therefore, if both implacable opponents and close allies are Muslims, it is imperative to begin to understand Islam.

The means of ensuring that we as an international community overcome the false and real confrontations between our faiths is through dialogue and understanding. Dr. Jill Carroll's book *A Dialogue of Civilizations* advocates the position of dialogue and I strongly endorse it. Dr. Carroll has done us all a great service by enlightening us about the unique Muslim philosophy of M. Fethullah Gülen. Gülen, a great Sufi Turkish leader, a pioneer of interfaith dialogue for over thirty years, believes that "dialogue is not a superfluous endeavor, but an imperative… that dialogue is among the duties of Muslims to make our world a more peaceful and safer place." At a period of time when humanity is in need of spiritual leaders, we have found such a leader in Fethullah Gülen. Gülen has spent his adult life voicing the cries and laments, as well as the beliefs and aspirations, of Muslims and of humanity in general. He has inspired an immense civil society movement that since the late 1960s has evolved and grown to encompass many facets of social life. Gülen as a Sufi Islamic intellectual and scholar has inspired millions, Muslim and non-Muslim alike, into service for humanity.

Within this text Dr. Jill Carroll continues the tradition of dialogue by presenting us with a textual dialogue between the thoughts and teachings of Gülen and five internationally known philosophers within the general humanities discourse: Immanuel Kant, Confucius, John Stuart Mill, Jean Paul Sartre, and Plato. Dr. Carroll is not only able to create a discourse reflecting the teachings of Gülen but also provides us with an example of the type of dialogue needed in the twenty-first century, one where thoughts and ideas wholly different from our own are presented before us in a rational thought-provoking manner.

There is no one more qualified to craft this textual dialogue than Dr. Carroll. As Associate Director of the Boniuk Center for the Study and Advancement of Religious Tolerance at Rice University and frequent writer and speaker on Gülen's ideas, she has acquired an acute understanding of his teachings. Coupled with her scholarly background as a professor of the humanities and comparative religion, she has gained an expertise in continental philosophy of religion which has enabled her with the skills to excel at this undertaking. Dr. Carroll has done much to present the Islamic ideals and principles of the Gülen movement to the larger community of scholars. I witnessed her devotion to the ideals of tolerance and dialogue as she lectured at the 2006 International Conference on Islam in the Contemporary World: The Fethullah Gülen Movement in Thought and Practice at the University of Oklahoma, where I was fortunate enough to participate as keynote speaker.

While conducting a research project for the Brookings Institution entitled "Islam in the Age of Globalization" during the spring of 2006, I traveled to nine Muslim countries, and my research team and I were shown just how influential Fethullah Gülen has become. In an attempt to understand the "mind" of Muslims throughout the Muslim world, we prepared a questionnaire that asked direct personal questions to each participant. The questions posed attempted to gauge reactions towards the West and globalization. We found that many people are following those who seek to put barriers around Islam, and to exclude everything else, especially Western influence. This idea is rapidly gaining popularity across the Muslim world. In Turkey, however, we saw that the most popular contemporary role model was Fethullah Gülen, indicating to us the importance of his intellectual movement and also its potential as a countervailing force to ideas of exclusion that are gaining more traction within the Muslim world.

The size and effectiveness of the Gülen movement has grown exponentially over the past thirty years. It now includes the establishment of hundreds of modern schools and several universities inside and outside of Turkey, a media network (two national TV channels, a weekly news magazine, and a leading daily newspaper), and business organizations. The movement has grown not as a political movement but as a social and spiritual one. As a unique social reformer, Gülen has introduced a new style of education that begins to integrate scientific knowledge and spiritual values. With this he is able to find an Islamic middle ground that stands in a critical engagement with modernity. He believes the real goal of nations is the renewal or "civilization" of individuals and society through moral action.

Gülen has drawn much inspiration from the teachings and writings of Mawlana Jalal al-Din Rumi and his messages of service to God and love and service to one another. Rumi, a best-selling author not only in the Muslim world but in the United States as well, intellectually and spiritually paved the way for the Gülen movement. Both men have devoted their lives to their understanding of Sufism. Gülen describes Rumi with great reverence, "not a pupil, a dervish, a representative or a master as is known amongst traditional Sufis. He developed a new method colored with revivalism, and personal individual reasoning by taking the Qur'an, the Sunnah, and Islamic piety as his reference points. With a new voice and breath, he successfully brought both those of his generation and those of times to follow to a new divine table."

Gülen helps us answer the questions of life, values, and the components of a just human society through reconciling the apparent differences between the positive sciences and divinity. In his writings and oral presentations, Gülen provides a guiding light for those seeking solutions to the dilemmas of today. He explains to us that the days of getting things done through brute force are over; it is by persuasion and the use of convincing argument that you get others to accept your ways. Only through cooperative understanding and respect can communities coexist in peace. Within our ever-shrinking world this lesson must be learned. Respect for cultural and religious customs has become compulsory. It is therefore essential that we create, by any and all means, a process of mutual understanding and interfaith dialogue. In this post-9/11 world of real and perceived "clash," the millions participating in the Gülen movement continue to provide us with both spiritual and practical guidance towards peace and tolerance of others. In a world where the most prominent Muslim leaders speak of conflict and confrontation, Gülen provides us with a "new voice" that calls people of all faiths to the "divine table." Through his guidance we can create a world where dialogue is our first course of action and confrontation is our very last. In this spirit, Dr. Carroll has contributed a work that enhances not only our understanding of Gülen's principles and teachings but brings attention to a philosophical movement that is truly significant in our time.

I would like to acknowledge Muhammed Çetin, President of the Institute for Interfaith Dialog, who initiated this important work for promoting dialogue and understanding between the West and the Muslim world, and also express my gratitude to David Montez for his assistance in preparing this foreword and commitment to dialogue. As someone actively involved in interfaith dialogue, I am very concerned with the need for understanding and compassion in this perilous time. As professor on campus I am in a unique position to witness the power of dialogue within the classroom and how it can change perspectives. As a father and a grandfather, the vital need for dialogue weighs upon me personally. The need to build bridges is crucial in ensuring the security of our children. Dialogue and understanding are no longer an intellectual pastime; they are an imperative if we are to survive the twenty-first century.

Professor Akbar Ahmed
Ibn Khaldun Chair of Islamic Studies
American University, Washington D.C.

INTRODUCTION

In December 2004, I traveled to Turkey for ten days as the guest of the Institute for Interfaith Dialog (IID) based in Houston, Texas. With me were about twenty other professors, clergy, and community leaders from Texas, Oklahoma, and Kansas. None of us had been to Turkey before, and none of us really knew what to expect. Each of us, in one way or another, had been approached by one or more Turkish young men at school, church, or somewhere else in the community and asked if we would travel on an interfaith dialogue trip to Turkey as a guest of their organization. Some of us got to know a few of the young men and their wives a little better by having dinner at their homes or by attending community fast-breaking dinners that IID sponsored during Ramadan. All of us had accepted the invitation based on our sense that these young men, their wives, and the organization were trustworthy.

What I did not know as I began the trip, but soon came to learn, was that the founders and volunteers at IID, and the organizers of our trip both in the United States and in Turkey were all members of a transnational community of people inspired by the ideas of a Turkish Islamic scholar named Fethullah Gülen. Gülen's sermons and lectures have circulated throughout Turkey and beyond for several decades now since he became a state-authorized preacher in 1958 and was appointed to a post in Izmir in south-western Turkey. We visited many of the schools, a hospital, and an interfaith organization founded by people in the Gülen movement. We shared meals with Turkish families in their homes and, on each occasion, I asked our hosts how they had come to hear of Gülen's ideas and what particularly had inspired them to get involved in the movement. They all gave essentially the same answer. The older people had been living in Izmir when Gülen began his ministry and were impressed and convinced by his message of education and altruism. Younger people with school-aged children came to know of the movement through nearby schools, which have excellent educational reputations, and became committed to the vision of global peace and progress through education and interfaith dialogue. A few others had been students themselves at schools founded by people in the Gülen movement and were now supporting the schools and other interfaith work in various ways as sponsors. In each case, the person had been touched deeply by Gülen's message and vision, and had committed to spreading it in the world.

I returned to Houston, the home base of IID, and deepened my relationship with the organization. The Boniuk Center for the Study and Advancement of Religious Tolerance at Rice University, for which I work, hosted a conference in November 2005 on Gülen's ideas which was attended by scholars from the United States, Europe, and Central Asia. We have collaborated with IID on a number of other projects, lectures, and panel events. I returned to Turkey again in May 2005 and July 2006 and met more people from the Gülen movement, increasing my understanding of Gülen's ideas and the impact they have on individuals in Turkey and on Turkey itself. Since my first trip to Turkey I have read much of Gülen's translated work and have had a great many conversations with my Turkish friends about his work. I am far from an expert on Gülen's ideas, on modern Turkish history, or on Sufism. I am, however, a specialist in religious studies (continental philosophy of religion), a comparativist in world religions, as well as a generalist in the discipline of the humanities. I have taught generalist, or "survey," courses in humanities in both undergraduate and graduate curricula for nearly fifteen years. These courses include world comparative literature, ethics, ancient and classical philosophy, modern political philosophy, as well as "great books" courses in both western and eastern historical, philosophical, religious, and literary traditions. My generalist competency extends to "eastern" thought as well as the "western," largely because of my specialty in religious philosophy. Consequently, when I first began reading Gülen's sermons and articles in translation, bells began ringing in my mind because of the deep connections I see between his work and that of some of the great thinkers and philosophers of world intellectual history.

My task in this book is to place the ideas of Fethullah Gülen into the context of the larger humanities. Specifically, I seek to create a textual dialogue between printed versions of selected articles, sermons, or speeches by Gülen, on the one hand, and the texts of selected thinkers, writers, philosophers, or theorists from general humanities discourse, on the other. These individuals from the humanities include Confucius, Plato, Immanuel Kant, John Stuart Mill, and Jean Paul Sartre. The location of their respective ideas within the larger discipline of humanities, as opposed to the sciences, prompts me to identify these figures, including Gülen, as humanistic thinkers, even though such a designation may be seen as problematic, depending on the definition of "humanism." In this work, I choose the broadest possible definition of humanism, a definition that does not view it as the necessary antithesis to a religious or theistic worldview. Professional philosophers and intellectual historians have identified as "humanism" or "humanistic" ideas and systems of thought that extend to antiquity, to as far back as Protagoras, who famously said "man is the measure of all things." Protagoras was not an atheist, nor were any of the other classical Greek philosophers who, during the fifth century BCE, shifted their focus of inquiry away from questions about the nature and components of the cosmos (air, water, substance, etc.) toward questions of the meaning of life, human values, the nature of the good life, and the components of a just human society. These concerns are those commonly and broadly identified with humanism or humanistic thinking, and many philosophies and worldviews, both religious and non-religious, qualify as humanistic in this regard.

Renaissance humanism, retrieving ideas from the classical world, moves its focus away from God toward humanity. In general, however, humanists of this period were not atheists, nor did they promote atheism as a tenet of their "humanistic" perspective. The focus on human ability and achievement, accompanied by a less interventionist view of God, simply opened the way for a scientific viewpoint to arise in the West which empowered humans to discover the laws of the universe, which were themselves created by God. European thinkers of this period, of course, came to this perspective within the larger theological rubric of Christianity and were indebted to Muslim scholars of immediately previous generations who had already defined the cutting edge of medicine, astronomy, mathematics, botany, and many other scientific disciplines inside their own theological rubric of Islam. In both instances, the humanism does not occur as a trumpeting of human power over God or against God's power. On the contrary, human beings provide witness and praise to God's power when they use their God-given capacities to uncover the mysteries of the universe that God created and use that knowledge for the progress and betterment of all human society. So, this form of humanism in no way undermines belief in God or religion. In fact, Muslim scholars, and later Christian scholars, are the chief examples of this broad form of pietistic humanism.

Of course, other forms of humanism are completely secular or atheistic. In the post-Renaissance modern period, subdivisions within larger humanism have emerged which specifically reject a religious or supernatural worldview, even to the point of being hostile to religion. Secular humanism is an atheistic subdivision of humanism that is incompatible with a religious viewpoint to a large extent. Neither Gülen, nor any other religious thinker, can be called a humanist inside this narrow definition of humanism. Nor could Kant, Mill, or Confucius; all of these men are routinely referred to as humanists and their ideas as forms of humanism, yet none of them are atheists. Clearly, then, the narrow, secular, atheistic definition of modern humanism is not the operative definition in this book.[1]

Therefore, I use a broader definition of humanism in this book, one that accounts more accurately than modern iterations for its long history and for the extraordinary achievements in religion, philosophy, literature, ethics, art, architecture, science, and mathematics that human beings have accomplished under its central rubric, the focus on or belief in human importance, power, status, and authority, a belief which in no way contradicts the central tenets or history of the three great monotheisms. Given this, I group Gülen with these other humanistic thinkers because his work, like theirs, focuses on central issues of human existence that have long been part of humanistic discourse in both its religious and non-religious forms. In other words, these thinkers are concerned with basic questions about the nature of human reality, the good human life, the state, and morality. Moreover, they reach similar conclusions regarding many of these issues and questions after deliberating about them from within their own traditions and cultural contexts.

In claiming similarity here, I am not asserting "sameness." These thinkers come from a vast diversity of backgrounds, time periods, cultural and national contexts, religious and spiritual traditions and more. They differ from each other in significant ways, to the point that in certain passages of their respective work, they denounce each other (in the case of the more recent writers) or, one could imagine, they would denounce each other on many points if they were in a real dialogue (not merely a "constructed" one). Gülen critiques outright Sartre, existentialists, and other atheists many times throughout his work. While I limit myself in this book to placing each of these thinkers in textual conversation only with Gülen, not with each other, one could imagine the conversations their major differences would generate. Mill argues for a kind of freedom that Plato would find abhorrent in his ideal republic. Conversely, Mill probably would find Plato's ideal republic an oppressive tyranny in most ways. Sartre's work blasts any notion of a "heaven of ideas," utterly universal and transcendent, whether it be articulated by Plato, Kant, or Gülen. Confucius, coming from a sixth-century Chinese perspective, has little in common with ideas from Western Enlightenment or post-Enlightenment thinkers like Kant or Mill.

Dialogue between people with vastly different worldviews, however, is what interests me. Moreover, I believe that such dialogue is vital in today's world, where globalization, mass communications, and technology have pushed individuals and groups together in ways never before seen in human history. People living in the twenty-first century interact with and are impacted more than ever before by other people and groups very different from them. We are increasingly confronted by people and groups whose worldviews are utterly different from ours, and these people are our neighbors, co-workers, schoolmates of our children, our in-laws, our clients, our employers, and more. Often, we may try to minimize our contact with those who are different from us, so that we do not have to extend ourselves outside comfortable boundaries. We may isolate ourselves and craft the arc of our lives into familiar orbits of peo-ple who look, think, speak, believe, and pray like us, but such iso-lation or minimizing of difference is not workable over time. In today's world of global connectedness, we must develop the capac-ity to dialogue and create relatedness with people vastly different from us. Part of that project involves finding ideas, beliefs, purpos-es, projects, and so forth, on which we can achieve resonance with each other. That is we do not need to be the same, but we should find just enough similarity between us that, for a certain distance down the road, we can hold hands as fellow travelers in this life, all the while mindful of our differences in myriad ways.

Gülen, in his career as a state-authorized preacher in Turkey and as an inspirational scholar and teacher to people throughout Turkey and beyond, has championed dialogue as a necessary com-mitment and activity in the contemporary world. Therefore, it is appropriate to place Gülen, via his texts, "in dialogue" with other thinkers and writers coming from very different perspectives from his. Such a project models for us as readers a way of becoming comfortable with difference. More importantly, though, such a dia-logue among individuals renowned for their knowledge and gifts can help all of us who care about such things to focus more deeply on the enduringly great issues of human life. While human lives in their particularities change era to era, the deep nature of human life, and the questioning and anxiety it provokes, has not changed. We ask today the same kinds of questions as our ancestors about the meaning of existence, the value of human life, how we are to set up society, and what the limits of freedom are. My hope is that this mock interaction between Gülen and the others listed above provides an opportunity for us, on whose shoulders the future rests, to take seriously our charge to create ourselves, society, and the world according the highest and best possible ideals.

I have organized the dialogues between Gülen and other thinkers around five major themes that capture central issues and concerns about human life in the world. These themes are: (1) inherent human value and moral dignity; (2) freedom; (3) ideal humanity; (4) education; and (5) responsibility. These themes are well-known to any students of general humanistic discourse, whether from the ancient period or the modern, whether from Europe, Asia, or Africa, whether from a religious or secular worldview. In each theme, I have identified a primary thinker to pair with Gülen in a textual interaction. I have chosen the primary thinkers based on the resonance their particular expression of the specific theme has with Gülen's expression of that same theme from within his Islamic perspective. I could have chosen other thinkers and fared just as well, probably, in terms of finding powerful expression of classic, enduring ideas and resonance with Gülen on these ideas. I chose the ones below because I felt they were particularly adept in their expression and, frankly, because of my deep admiration and respect for their work, having taught their ideas in college classrooms now for fifteen years. Moreover, these conversations discuss themes which I believe are of the utmost importance for our scholarly and civic consideration.

The chapters are connected to each other thematically and refer to one another on certain points. Such references, however, are minimal and the chapters mostly are freestanding. Readers may read the chapters in any order they wish, or only the chapters that interest them, without losing any of the coherence of the book. Readers who do this will not be "lost" in the text. Moreover, I have written this book for a more general audience than most scholarly books target. I do not assume that readers have read Kant, Sartre, Confucius, Plato, Mill, or even Gülen, for that matter. I do not spend any time providing biographical information on these authors. Such information is readily available to readers from a variety of sources. My goal in the book is to explain the ideas of these thinkers, as I interpret them, as clearly as possible for an audience of generally educated people who may or may not have a background in the humanities as it is studied in the West. For this reason, I have chosen to overlook many details and subtleties that, were I writing a more traditional scholarly book, would exhaust a great many pages and textual footnotes. As it is, I hope I have written an informative, substantial, and interesting book that people who are interested in the history of ideas, global intellectual history, and cross-cultural dialogue will find useful and even inspiring.

1

Gülen and Kant on Inherent Human Value and Moral Dignity

The very word "humanism" places the human—the individual, the group of individuals, the species, the form of being—at the center of its concerns. Therefore, humanism's long claim is that human life in general, and human lives in particular, have some form of inherent human value. Moreover, respect for this inherent human value, in many humanistic systems, forms the starting point or grounding for fundamental morality. No one articulates this more powerfully and coherently than eighteenth century German philosopher Immanuel Kant. In his *Grounding for the Metaphysics of Morals*, first published in 1785, Kant attempts to articulate "the supreme principle of morality."[1]

He intends to articulate this principle in completely rational, not empirical, terms in order to prevent moral actions from being dependent on circumstances, human feelings, whims, or conditions. Time and space here do not suffice to consider the merits of Kant's method or conclusions with regards to rational versus empirical ethics, or to summarize adequately the bulk of his arguments. Therefore, we will focus on those points most relevant to his discussion of human beings as ends in themselves and, as such, possessors of inherent value that must not be maligned.

Kant's argument in the *Grounding* centers on three core concepts: reason, will, and duty. These three concepts are bound together in a very specific way, and he moves logically from one to the next in order to set up the context for his ethical philosophy. He begins with the will. The will, particularly a good will, is required for any notion of morality. Kant asserts this immediately in the first section of his essay:

> There is no possibility at all of thinking of anything at all in the world, or even out of it, which can be regarded as good without qualification, except a good will. Intelligence, wit, judgment, and whatever talents of the mind one might want to name are doubtless in many respects good and desirable, as are such qualities of temperament as courage, resolution, perseverance. But they can also become extremely bad and harmful if the will, which is to make use of these gifts of nature and which in its special constitution is called character, is not good . . . The sight of a being who is not graced by a touch of a pure and good will but who yet enjoys an uninterrupted prosperity can never delight a rational and impartial spectator. Thus a good will seems to constitute the indispensable condition of being even worthy of happiness.[2]

Nothing good is even possible, then, without a good will, regardless of whatever other talents or capacities a person may possess. The good will is like a basic character state and is indispensable for moral action. Kant continues his analysis by moving to the concept of reason. Reason, in his view, separates humans from animals in a general way, but more specifically reason functions in humans in a way that illumines a more fundamental difference between humans and other living beings. Kant operates on the principle that nature designs the constitution of every organized being such that no organ exists in it that does not fulfill a purpose that it alone is designed to fulfill to the highest and best possibility. In other words, every organ has a purpose and it fulfills that purpose better than any other organ in the living being. Kant identifies reason as a kind of organ and asks what its purpose is for human living. He says:

> Now if that being's preservation, welfare, or in a word its happiness, were the real end of nature in the case of being having reason and will, then nature would have hit upon a very poor

arrangement in having the reason of the creature carry out this
purpose. For all the actions which such a creature has to perform with this purpose in view, and the whole rule of his conduct would have been prescribed much more exactly by
instinct: and the purpose in question could have been attained
much more certainly by instinct than it ever can be by reason.[3]

Here, Kant asserts that the achieving of happiness defined as
our preservation or welfare is not the function of reason in human
beings or beings who possess will and reason. Welfare, preservation, or happiness can be achieved by instinct as much as or even
better than by reason, as it is in animals. Therefore, Kant says that
"existence has another and much more worthy purpose, for which,
and not for happiness, reason is quite properly intended."[4] Kant
concludes that reason's purpose is to develop the good will. He
says, "Reason recognizes as its highest practical function the establishment of a good will, whereby in the attainment of this end reason is capable only of its own kind of satisfaction."[5]

What is the good will? How is it to be defined? In short, Kant
defines the good will in human beings as the ability to act from
duty alone and not according to any circumstances or sentiment.
This definition alerts us to perhaps Kant's chief concern in his essay,
and that is to find a firm grounding for morality. In his view, moral
systems that focus on pleasure, happiness, or sentiments do not
provide a sufficient grounding for ethics because they are transient
and subject to many variables in human life. Our sentiments may
change depending on circumstances. What gave us pleasure for-
merly may cease to bring pleasure. In the realm of mundane life
and property, these variables have minimal consequence. In the
realm of morality, however, they can have tremendous consequences.
Inasmuch as morality guides our actions toward people, our guiding principles can change with our mood, whims, or circumstances
if they are rooted in sentiment or pleasure; we may not feel like
telling the truth or being compassionate or fair in our dealings with
people. For Kant, to ground morality on feelings or pleasure is to build
our house on sinking sand and, thus, to risk everything. Therefore,
Kant seeks a more secure foundation for morality, and he believes

he can find it in reason, will, and duty properly understood as they work together in human life.

So, in summary, for Kant there is no possibility for good without the good will, and reason exists in us to develop that will, which is the ability of humans to act from duty alone regardless of feelings, circumstances, or pleasure to be gained. Kant spends most of his treatise explaining these three core concepts of reason, will, and duty, and their operation in a metaphysics of morals from which human beings can codify a supreme principle of morality to guide all deliberations and actions. This supreme principle is called the categorical imperative, which takes several forms in the treatise, the most common being "I should never act except in such a way that I can also will that my maxim should become a universal law."[6]

What does all this have to do with inherent human value? For Kant, humans, as rational beings, are possessors in their nature of the very grounding of morality and, as such, have inherent value. Outside of human beings as rational agents, there is no practical notion of the moral good, since there is no being that can determine it rationally and apply it universally other than human beings. A rational being is a being who, from within himself, determines what is the universal moral law. Such a being, who generates principles of value, is in himself a value or good. In Kant's words, "rational nature exists as an end in itself."[7]

Indeed, Kant delineates a version of the categorical imperative that centers on this: "Act in such a way that you treat humanity, whether in your own person or in the person of another, always at the same time as an end and never simply as a means."[8] He envisions a "kingdom of ends," that is, a community organized around these moral principles in which human beings, as rational agents and ends in themselves, legislate universal moral law, always with a view of humans as ends in themselves, not only means. Inside Kant's kingdom of ends, things either have a price or a dignity, a market value, or an inherent worth. Kant explains:

> Whatever has a price can be replaced by something else as its equivalent; on the other hand, whatever is above all price, and

> therefore admits of no equivalent, has a dignity. Whatever has reference to general human inclinations and needs has a market price; . . . but that which constitutes the condition under which alone something can be an end in itself has not merely a relative worth, i.e. a price, but has an intrinsic worth, i.e. a dignity. Now morality is the condition under which alone a rational being can be an end in himself, for only thereby can he be a legislating member in the kingdom of ends. Hence morality and humanity, insofar as it is capable of morality, alone have dignity. Skill and diligence in work have a market price; wit, lively imagination, and humor have an affective price; but fidelity to promises and benevolence based on principles (not on instinct) have intrinsic worth.[9]

Human value is not negotiable; it is not a thing bought or sold, or something relative in value depending on market conditions. Kant's formulation of human being allows the human disposition to "be recognized as dignity and puts it infinitely beyond all price, with which it cannot in the least be brought into competition or comparison without, as it were, violating its sanctity."[10] He goes on to say that "[r]ational nature is distinguished from the rest of nature by the fact that it sets itself an end."[11] Therefore, another dimension of the categorical imperative is that "a rational being himself must be made the ground for all maxims of actions and must thus be used never merely as means but as the supreme limiting condition in the use of all means, i.e., always at the same time as an end."[12]

As indicated above, human beings are ends in themselves, not merely a means to someone else's end. They cannot be used only as a tool to secure another's goal, agenda, or ideology. While humans may be employed in those efforts, they cannot be treated as merely employees of a project. They are always at the same time an end in themselves, bearers of inherent value and dignity, regardless of any advantage or benefit they provide to anyone else's projects or agendas.

In making these claims, Kant makes radical statements for his time. In a sense, he is furthering a particular conversation in the West that began a generation or so earlier with philosophers like

John Locke, who argued for a governmental structure not rooted in the divine right of a monarchy but in the sovereign will of the governed, that is, the people of the political community. The only way such arguments become conceivable and logically consistent is if significant worth is accorded to human beings *as humans*. Important to note, also, is that Kant's articulation of human worth is not a religiously grounded one, although Kant himself was a Christian. Locke's arguments are not Christian, either, despite his own faith. Both are concerned to base their arguments for human worth in non-religious terms in order to make them as immune as possible from what they saw as the whims of religion. We must remember that both men lived during periods of religious wars throughout Europe when people were put to death because their religion differed from that of the monarch who ruled by divine right and against whom people had no recourse for a redress of grievances. Moreover, Kant is well aware of the emotionalism that often accompanies religion and, thus, does not view religious faith as a stable enough grounding for moral principles, which include the inherent dignity of all people. He wrote an entire book called *Religion Within the Limits of Reason Alone* in which he tried to extract religious practice and conviction from pious feelings and inclinations and, instead, tie it exclusively to the cultivation of a moral character and to principled ethical action. His overriding concern across his work is to underscore in the most universal way possible, which he sees as through reason which all humans possess, the inherent worth of human beings so that stable morality is possible in the world regardless of the contingencies of life, including changes of rulership, conversion to new religions, personal tastes, and the like.

The Western Enlightenment, of which Kant was a part, championed these notions of inherent human dignity which brought about radical social changes in the eighteenth century and beyond. Of course, these ideas are not unique to the Western Enlightenment; thinkers and writers from many parts of the world articulate such notions from within their own cultural, religious, or philosophical rubrics. Islamic scholars, for example, for centuries and from many parts of the world, have interpreted the Qur'an as expressing such notions about inherent human value and moral dignity. Gülen's work is an example of Islamic scholarship that emphasizes the Qur'anic "voice" insisting upon the distinct beauty and worth of human beings. Indeed, Gülen finds in the Qur'an and other Islamic sources strong claims about human dignity in the first place; he does not bring such claims to the Qur'an after having determined them through other means or from other sources. Gülen repeatedly references portions of the Qur'an when responding to questions about *jihad*, violence, terror, and respect for human life in general (not just Muslim life). In these sections of his work, Gülen's resonance with the ideas of Kant becomes clear, although they most certainly develop their respective expressions of inherent human value and moral dignity from entirely different perspectives.

Gülen throughout his work speaks of the transcendent value of human beings. He begins one piece with a powerful statement:

> Humans, the greatest mirror of the names, attributes, and deeds of God, are a shining mirror, a marvelous fruit of life, a source for the whole universe, a sea that appears to be a tiny drop, a sun formed as a humble seed, a great melody in spite of their insignificant physical positions, and the source for existence all contained within a small body. Humans carry a holy secret that makes them equal to the entire universe with all their wealth of character; a wealth that can be developed to excellence.[13]

He continues by claiming that "[a]ll of existence becomes a legible book only with their [human] understanding and foresight . . . humans—together with everything in and around them—. . . are the royal witnesses of their Master."[14] He finishes this line of thinking in the section by saying, "[w]hen this entire boundless universe, with all of its riches, components, and history, is connected to humanity it becomes clear why the value of humankind transcends all . . . According to Islam, humans are superior merely because they are humans."[15] So, in these passages, Gülen claims the greatest value for human beings, as opposed to angels or animals, because of their capacity as witnesses and interpreters of the universe. As such witnesses, they are the mirrors of certain aspects of God, the reflectors of the divine book of the universe. Without them, the universe is not known, nor is there anyone to know it.

Elsewhere, Gülen reiterates that human beings are the center and meaning of the universe and that, as such, they possess value higher even than angels. Humans, through their activities and understandings, give life its essence. He says:

> The human being is the essence and vital element of being, the index and core element of the universe. Human beings are at the center of creation; all other things, living or non-living, compose concentric circles around them . . . Taking into account all the honor that has been granted to humanity, compared with all the rest of creation, humanity must be seen as the voice that expresses the nature of things, the nature of events and, of course, the nature of the All-Powerful One Who is behind everything, as well as being understood as a heart that encompasses all the universes. With human beings, creation has found its interpreter and matter has been distilled through the cognition of people, finding its spiritual meaning. The monitoring of things is an ability peculiar to human beings, their being able to read and interpret the book of the universe is a privilege, and their attribution of everything to the Creator is an exceptional blessing. Their quiet introspection is contemplation, their speech is wisdom, and their conclusive interpretation of all things is love.[16]

So, whereas Kant argues for the inherent value of human beings based on their being rational agents through whom the moral law comes into practical being in the world, Gülen argues for the value of human beings based on their position as the only agents through whom God's book of creation can be known and the wonders of existence expressed. In both instances, human beings, as individuals and as groups, are indispensable to fundamental constituents of existence, in one case morality through their rationality, in the other all knowledge, wisdom, and love through their being mirrors of the names and attributes of God.

Moreover, Gülen, like Kant, takes human value and dignity as the basis for defining legitimate and illegitimate behaviors toward people in society, although Gülen grounds his claims in the Qur'an, not in reason alone, unlike Kant. In a piece addressing human rights in Islam, he argues that Islam has the highest conception of universal human rights and that it has not been surpassed by any other religion, system, or commission. He says, "Islam accepts the killing of one person as if all of humanity had been killed, for the murder of one person allows the idea that any person can be killed."[17] Gülen qualifies this statement in a way common to most religious and philosophical thinkers, namely, that it perhaps is justified to kill those who are killing others, those trying to destroy society, and so on. In these instances, the killing is not murder; it is punishment or self-defense. Elsewhere, he says that in the Islamic view:

> A human being, be they man or woman, young or old, white or black, is respected, protected and inviolate. Their belongings cannot be taken away, nor can their chastity be touched. They cannot be driven out of their native land, and their independence cannot be denied. They cannot be prevented from living in accordance with their principles, either. Moreover, they are prohibited from committing such crimes against others as well. They do not have the right to inflict harm on this gift [of humanity] that is presented to them by God, for they only are in temporary possession of this bounty; God is the true owner of everything . . . Humans are to defend and keep safe this gift. It is holy for them; they will not harm it, nor allow it to come to any harm. When necessary they will fight for it and die for it.[18]

Gülen here again ascribes human worth to God. Humanity or human beingness is a gift that cannot be transgressed or fouled. As such, it is the basis for obligatory positive actions, like protecting people and keeping them safe, as well as prohibitions against harmful actions, such as harming people or stealing their property. Gülen sees these harmful actions as being in direct opposition to the spirit of love, which he identifies as the central heart of Islam. He says:

> Actually, love is the rose in our belief, a realm of the heart that never withers. Above all else, just as God wove the universe like a lace on the loom of love, the most magical and charming music in the bosom of existence is always love.[19]

This love translates into a basic humanism in which people develop love within themselves for others and for all creation and show that love by support and service to the world. This is at the heart of Islam, Gülen says. Unfortunately, however, this idea has either been ignored or perverted. He explains:

> Humanism is a doctrine of love and humanity which is interpreted recklessly these days, and it has a potential to be easily manipulated through different interpretations . . . It should be difficult to reconcile with humanism the strange behavior of championing "pity and mercy" for those who are involved in anarchy and terror to demolish the unity of a country, for those who have heartlessly murdered innocent people as a part of centuries-long activities that are aimed at destroying the welfare of a nation, and even more horribly, for those who do this in the name of religious values, and those who recklessly accuse Islam of allowing terrorist attacks.[20]

Gülen here points to the deep hypocrisy and violence in many modernist movements that claim to be humanist, and he mentions, in passing, those who do similar horrible things in the name of religion. In both instances, what becomes lost is the true "doctrine of love and humanity" which grounds both of them in their true, authentic forms. Islam, then, in his view, shares with *true* humanism a commitment to love of humanity, the difference being that Islam gleans this commitment from the revelation of the Qur'an, whereas humanistic philosophy derives it from other sources or modes.

Clearly, Gülen echoes the spirit of Kantian analysis despite coming from a completely different framework, namely, the religio-philosophical worldview of Islam. The inherent value, even holiness, of humanity demands universal protection and categorically forbids any transgression of it. In the West, the ideas of Kant (and of Locke) about inherent human dignity and basic rights find their political manifestation in the liberal democracy of the modern nation-state. Muslim societies have actualized their commitment to human dignity in other ways. Despite the differences here between the West and Muslim countries, Gülen sees no inherent incompatibility between Islam and democracy in general; the basic commitments to human beings and their essential rights, albeit grounded in different starting points (one religious, the other secular) cohere with one another. Gülen, however, argues that Islam can improve democracy in important respects. Democracy in the modern period, he says, has been wedded to problematic philosophies, such as dialectical materialism and historicism, which he views as fatalistic. Also, democracies can engender a rugged individualism that undermines the health of the whole society, although Gülen asserts that in Islam "[a]ll rights are important, and the rights of the individual cannot be sacrificed for the sake of society."[21] In the end, Gülen says, Islam is a comprehensive set of religiously derived principles that can guide democracy as it continues to develop and improve. He explains:

> Democracy has developed over time. Just as it has gone through many different stages in the past, it will continue to evolve and improve in the future. Along the way, it will be shaped into a more humane and just system, one based on righteousness and reality. If human beings are considered as a whole, without disregarding the spiritual dimension of their existence and their spiritual needs, and without forgetting that human life is not limited to this mortal life and that all people have a great craving for eternity, democracy could reach the peak of perfection and bring even more happiness to humanity. Islamic principles of equality, tolerance, and justice can help it to do just this.[22]

Clearly, Gülen sees shortcomings in democracy that Islam can address, particularly on issues of humanity and how human beings are understood. Democracy tends to ignore the spiritual dimensions of life itself and of human nature—traits that demand universal respect and even awe of human beings. Kant might question Gülen on this, if for no other reason than to root all society, including systems of justice and morality, in a religious worldview, is to place it in the hands of something that, in Kant's view, ultimately cannot be proven rationally and certainly, falling as it does within the domain of conscience or faith, cannot be compelled without doing violence to the very humanity it seeks to defend and revere. On the other hand, Kant arguably would be pleased with the results of any religious worldview that ascribes ever more holiness and respect to human beings such that their intrinsic worth is held as a sacred Truth; he would simply say that such a worldview does not have as firm a foundation as he would like, rooted as it is in sentiments or ultimately unprovable faith.

Regardless, I think it is safe to say that claims of the inherent value of moral dignity of human beings, whether made by thinkers of the Western Enlightenment, by Islamic scholars interpreting the Qur'an, or by others from any tradition whatsoever are vital in today's world. The claims, in and of themselves, accomplish nothing. As history clearly shows, people may organize themselves under all manner of high and lofty banners such as "humanity," "human rights," "the common man," and proceed to commit atrocities and even genocides against the very human beings they claim to respect. Such is the deep hypocrisy and fallibility that plagues human life. When human beings truly and authentically commit themselves, however, to such claims and determine their actions by such claims, culture and society become less savage, bloody, and brute. History, in addition to showing us persecutions and genocides, also shows us that societies that keep inherent human value at the forefront of their political and cultural existence allow a measure of peace and stability for residents and citizens, and such societies have come in all eras and places of human history. When those same societies fall into persecutions and genocides, most often it is because they have abandoned the principles of inherent human value and moral dignity.

In affirming the inherent value and dignity of humanity, we also implicitly affirm the conditions that uphold and sustain that humanity. To value humanity is to commit to philosophical, spiritual, social, and political structures that cultivate that humanity and bring it through its own growth and development into its fullest actualization in individuals and groups. One of those conditions is freedom—the freedom to think, to learn, to express, and to live as one sees fit. This theme is the subject of our next chapter.

2

Gülen and Mill on Freedom

Humanistic thinking places freedom of thought and expression of ideas as a central plank of its platform, both philosophically and socio-politically. Free press, free and peaceful public protest, freedom of religion, the right to assemble, and other such institutions in the West all stem from the ideal of freedom articulated in modern humanisms, whereas in other parts of the world, including in Muslim lands, these freedoms stemmed from other sources. Philosophically, the ideal of freedom extends back to the ancient world as philosophers challenged themselves and others with all manner of ideas and sat debating them in the marketplace with anyone who would listen. Some of the greatest ideas of classical learning come from these philosophers who, even if they were put to death or exiled for their ideas eventually, allowed themselves to think and speak freely, refusing to shackle their minds and voices when the State commanded it.

In the modern West, several philosophers and writers powerfully express this ideal of freedom. In my view, however, none expresses this ideal more exhaustively and more radically than nineteenth century British social and political theorist John Stuart Mill. In this chapter, I place Mill into a dialogue with Gülen around the ideal of freedom of thought. Mill and Gülen are vastly different from each other in significant and obvious ways. Despite their different contexts and worldviews, both men articulate specific visions of society that at least theoretically would be tolerant in matters of religious belief and practice and would allow vigorous inquiry and debate on issues related to truth in most, perhaps all, domains. These similarities between their respective "societies" exist because of their common commitment to the ideal of freedom, especially in matters of thought and conscience.

Mill is perhaps most famous for *Utilitarianism*, his work of ethical philosophy, and I will refer to this work later in the chapter. First, however, I wish to focus on another of his important works, *On Liberty*, published in 1859. In this text, Mill sets his project as an articulation of social or civil liberty, that is, "the nature and limits of the power that can be legitimately exercised by society over the individual."[1] He explains that a recent previous generation in the West concerned itself with the tyranny of magistrates and, therefore, developed representative forms of government that threw off the despotic powers of divine right monarchs and the like. He and his generation are the beneficiaries of that struggle and, for the most part, no longer struggle against that kind of tyranny.

Rather, Mill asserts, the current generation, that is, his generation in nineteenth century Britain, must fight another kind of tyranny, the tyranny of the majority. Mill says:

> Protection, therefore, against the tyranny of the magistrate is not enough; there needs protection also against the tyranny of the prevailing opinion and feeling; against the tendency of society to impose, by other means than civil penalties, its own ideas and practices as rules of conduct on those who dissent from them; to fetter the development, and, if possible, prevent the formation, of any individuality not in harmony with its ways, and compel all characters to fashion themselves upon the model of its own. There is a limit to the legitimate interference of collective opinion with individual independence: and to find that limit, and maintain it against encroachment, is as indispensable to a good condition of human affairs, as protection against political despotism.[2]

In other words, Mill detects a subtle tyranny that exists in society even when representative government is in place. This tyranny is a social or civil tyranny, a pressure that society exerts on its members to conform to "normal" beliefs and practices in all parts of life simply because those are the "norm" and are practiced by the majority of people in the society. Therefore, says the logic of the majority, everyone should "toe the line," or be forced to do so. Mill rejects this tyranny and sets about to determine the principle by which we can determine the legitimate interference of the state or social agents with an individual's freedom, since mostly these determinations are made based purely on personal preference or custom. He states his principle of civic freedom early in the essay:

> [T]hat the sole end for which mankind are warranted, individually or collectively, in interfering with the liberty of action of any of their number, is self-protection. That the only purpose for which power can be rightfully exercised over any member of a civilized community, against his will, is to prevent harm to others. His own good, either physical or moral, is not a sufficient warrant . . . Over himself, over his body and mind, the individual is sovereign.[3]

This is a radical principle of freedom, one that probably no contemporary society implements consistently. It makes direct and measurable harm to others nearly the only legitimate grounds on which the state or civil authorities can interfere with an individual's actions. This principle is probably far too liberal for Gülen; for example, Islam, in general, forbids the taking of one's own life, so Mill's principle of freedom limited only by harm to others, not to oneself, is insufficient. Gülen, following Islamic teaching, would probably say that people do not have the freedom to harm themselves in the form of taking their own life. Nevertheless, resonance does exist between Gülen and Mill on this idea of freedom, particularly in the domain of thought and discussion, to which Mill devotes an entire chapter in his essay.

Mill unequivocally supports freedom of thought and discussion, even if the ideas expressed and discussed in society end up being false. He says an assertion made to the community for consideration exists either as true, false, or somewhere in between—a partial truth or partial falsehood. Regardless, societies' best interests are served when they allow free expression and discussion of ideas. If the idea is true, people will gain a fresh appreciation for its truth by discussing it, revisiting the arguments for its truth, and defending it against its detractors. In this way, the true ideas remain alive and vibrant for people instead of becoming stale and dormant from simply being accepted as true for generations. If the idea is false, society again benefits from the public discussion. Evidence of its falsehood is reviewed or made clear to everyone involved and, as a result, people can now embrace the truth more fully than before because of their fresh conviction. Most likely, Mill says, the idea expressed will be a mixture of truth and falsehood. Truly, no one has the full truth about anything; human minds cannot conceive truth in its entirety about anything, and certainly not about God or the Infinite, because we do not know things in themselves, but only our positional perceptions of things. Moreover, finite minds cannot conceive infinity. Therefore, all ideas should be expressed freely in society so that partial truths can be strengthened into fuller truths through the mechanism of civil engagement and debate.

The social benefits of free thought and discussion are clear enough, but Mill goes deeper into the actual impact that free thought has on individuals who make up society. Societies, especially with regard to religion, most often ban free thought and discussion in an effort to stop heresy, but such bans do not impact the heretics as much as they do everyone else. Mill says:

> The greatest harm done is to those who are not heretics, and whose whole mental development is cramped, and their reason cowed, by the fear of heresy. Who can compute what the world loses in the multitude of promising intellects combined with timid characters, who dare not follow out any bold, vigorous, independent train of thought, lest it should land them in something which would admit of being considered irreligious or immoral?[4]

Mill's point here is that overweening fears of heresy stamp out not only heretics but also those who have bold, new ideas to share about anything, including received traditions, even those considered sacred. When the threat of punishment for heresy is so strong in a society, or when a society threatens civil penalties on those who express ideas other than those expressly allowed by the civic "authorities," all of society suffers. Mental strength comes with practice and challenge. A society that clamps down on thought and discussion becomes weak and atrophied. Mill continues:

> No one can be a great thinker who does not recognize that as a thinker it is his first duty to follow his intellect to whatever conclusions it may lead. Truth gains more even by the errors of one who, with due study and preparation, thinks for himself, than by the true opinions of those who only hold them because they do not suffer themselves to think.[5]

Again, true ideas become stagnant and weak when not regularly challenged in debate and discussion. Those who espouse true ideas do not hold those truths honestly if they have not allowed themselves to think freely, which may mean questioning long-held truths. Mill claims, however, that the point is not merely to create individual thinkers. He says:

> Not that it is solely, or chiefly, to form great thinkers, that freedom of thinking is required. On the contrary, it is as much and even more indispensable to enable average human beings to attain the mental stature which they are capable of. There have been, and may again be, great individual thinkers in the general atmosphere of mental slavery. But there never has been, nor ever will be, in that atmosphere an intellectually active people.[6]

Here, we see Mill articulating the ideal of freedom for the most humanistic of reasons in addition to the utilitarian. Implied in this passage is a conviction that human beings are beings who think, who search for truth about myriad things from the most mundane to the most sublime, who create knowledge, and that these activities are part of what it means to be human. Freedom of thought, expression, and inquiry is vital not only for geniuses, who would never be able to share their genius for the benefit of society without the freedom to work; freedom is vital, perhaps even more so, for common people going about their lives, people of common intelligence, so that they can be intellectually active and engaged people. Of course, this provides a benefit to society and is, thus, a utilitarian or functional claim, but it also a humanistic claim because of what it holds for common people. People in general must be free to think, inquire, and to express because to do so is what it means to be human, and only when allowed to be fully human can we create a society geared for the human, as both an end and a means.

Here also, we can bring Gülen into the discussion, for he most often speaks of the ideal of freedom in both humanistic and utilitarian terms. Gülen often speaks in his work of freedom from tyranny. In many contexts, he is referring to the tyrannies various groups of Muslims have endured in recent years under powers of secularism and colonialism. In other contexts, however, he speaks in more universal terms about the freedom each individual has by virtue of being human. His views resonate with Mill's stated principle of liberty when he asserts that "[f]reedom allows people to do whatever they want, provided that they do not harm others and that they remain wholly devoted to the truth."[7] The last phrase— "that they remain wholly devoted to the truth" —might cause Mill some pause at first, but he might argue that even those lost in or committed to falsehoods are wholly devoted to truth; they are just wrong about the truth. To speak or act in a way not "wholly devoted to truth" could include, for Mill and Gülen both, things like slander, libel, or yelling "Fire!" in a crowded theater when there is no fire.

Gülen's championing of tolerance is inconceivable without a commitment to freedom of thought and discussion, mainly because tolerance is unnecessary if freedom of thought, discussion, personal choice, and so on, is not allowed. Tolerance is a virtue precisely because people are free and will choose different beliefs, religions, and pursuits. Gülen makes this point many times, often in discussions of democracy alone, or democracy and Islam, between which he sees no incompatibility whatsoever. In a piece on forgiveness, Gülen links tolerance and democracy through the concept of freedom. "Democracy is a system," he says, "that gives everyone who is under its wing the opportunity to live and express their own feelings and thoughts. Tolerance comprises an important dimension of this. In fact, it can be said that democracy is out of the question in a place where tolerance does not exist."[8]

Such statements, however, do not carry the radical edge of Mill's claims about the necessity of freedom and the protection people need from social tyranny. Only when Gülen exposits his notions of the ideal human beings, or the "inheritors of the earth" as he calls them in one work, do we see not only the deep commitment to freedom, but also the rationale for such a commitment, a truly humanistic rationale. In *The Statue of Our Souls*, he lays out a broad vision for a society and world led by individuals of spiritual, moral, and intellectual excellence. He calls these people "inheritors of the Earth"[9] and goes into some depth in describing their characters and attributes.* In his enumeration of their central traits, the fifth trait he identifies as "being able to think freely and being respectful to freedom of thought."[10] He continues:

> Being free and enjoying freedom are a significant depth of human willpower and a mysterious door through which man may set forth into the secrets of the self. One unable to set forth into that depth and unable to pass through that door can hardly be called human.[11]

So, freedom of thought is central to being human, to humanity itself. Without freedom of thought, not only as a social or political principle but also as an ability in oneself, one cannot really be called a human being. In other words, one does not reach human capacity without freedom of thought. Gülen elaborates:

> In circumstances in which restrictions have been imposed on reading, thinking, feeling and living, it is impossible to retain one's human faculties, let alone achieve renewal and progress. In such a situation it is quite difficult to maintain even the level of a plain and common man, let alone to raise great personalities

---

* I will discuss this concept of "inheritors of the earth" as well as Gülen's social vision in more depth in chapter 3.

> who leap with the spirit of renewal and reform, and whose eyes
> are on infinity. In such conditions there exist only weak charac-
> ters who experience deviations in their personalities and men of
> sluggish souls and paralyzed senses.[12]

Human development and, by extension, social development and growth—all reform and progress—depend on freedom of thought and living. A society without such freedom does not nurture the people of spirit and vision that lead it forward into new dimensions. Even worse, perhaps, such a society does not nurture common people to attain their fullest human capacities. Here, Gülen's ideas resonate with Mill's as he champions freedom for its usefulness to society and for its humanistic value. Indeed, the former is rooted in the latter; that is, freedom is beneficial to society because of the "work" it does in creating and developing human beings as individuals. As we saw in the previous section, human beings are of the highest value. It follows, then, that developing human capacity, or human "beingness," is of the highest value as well.

Gülen laments the recent history of Turkey and other Islamic regions where the populations have undergone, and sometimes continue to endure, social structures in which freedom of thought and learning are forbidden either through outright censure, or through dominant state-sponsored ideologies. Regarding the world of Islamic learning in particular he speaks of a vibrant past of scholarship and learning that was open to different fields of knowledge and scientific inquiry. In such a civilization, determinations concerning the proper boundaries for freedom were grounded in the *Sunnah** of the Prophet Muhammad and other such Islamic sources, which themselves accord high value to human freedom. That spirit of scholarship, however, gave way to narrowness and rote memorization of approved works. At that point, all human potential began its slow decay, easy prey for opportunistic tyrants, ideologues, and colonialists.

---

* The exemplary life of Prophet Muhammad and the set of norms he established for thinking, living, and worshiping in accordance with Islam.

He longs for a renewal among Muslims so that Islamic civilization can again take a place at the helm of global leadership, as it did
in past centuries when much of what constituted "civilization"
came from the Islamic world. In order for that to happen, he says:

> [W]e have to be more free-thinking and free-willed. We need
> those vast hearts who can embrace impartial free-thinking, who
> are open to knowledge, sciences, and scientific research, and
> who can perceive the accord between the Qur'an and the
> *Sunnatullah** in the vast spectrum from the universe to life.[13]

Without renewing a capacity for freedom of thought, both
individually and collectively, Islamic civilization, indeed all civilization, is lost. No possibility of authentic, robust humanity exists
without freedom of thought. No possibility of greatness in civilization exists without authentic humanity.

So, Gülen and Mill resonate with each other in many respects
on the vital role that freedom plays in society both in terms of its
own functioning and in terms of general humanistic commitment.
A society that oppresses free thought is not a thriving, working society, nor is it a society that values the human, no matter how it may
attempt to defend its oppression by appealing to human interest.

Now, however, I wish to address freedom, in both Mill and
Gülen, from a slightly different angle. This has to do with the quality of freedom that both allow for in their respective work. We will
see that the quality of freedom each claims for human beings is of
a type that only human beings possess and that therefore confirms
the special dignity that human beings have in the world, which is
reflected in humanistic discourse.

On the theme of freedom, Mill is most known for his essay *On
Liberty*, which is why I have focused on it in this chapter. His other major work is *Utilitarianism*, a work in ethical philosophy that
rejects Kantian ethics and attempts to articulate an ethical philosophy rooted in happiness or pleasure. Utilitarianism as a philosophy
predates Mill, of course, and goes by many names throughout history,

---

* *Sunnatullah* refers to the unchanging patterns of God's action in the universe.

including Epicureanism. The most common name for this during Mill's time was "the greatest happiness principle." Mill defines utilitarianism in his book:

> The creed which accepts as the foundation of morals "utility" or the "greatest happiness principle" holds that actions are right in proportion as they tend to promote happiness; wrong as they tend to produce the reverse of happiness. By happiness is intended pleasure and the absence of pain; by unhappiness, pain and the privation of pleasure . . . [P]leasure and freedom from pain are the only things desirable as ends; and . . . all desirable things (which are as numerous in the utilitarian as in any other scheme) are desirable either for the pleasure inherent in themselves or as means to the promotion of pleasure and the prevention of pain.[14]

In utilitarianism, as in ancient Epicureanism, pleasure and pain become the touchstones for what is good, to be desired, and ultimately for right and wrong. Mill here defines utilitarianism in a way completely consistent with the ancient Greek philosophy. He goes on to explain that, just like the ancient followers of Epicurus, he and other utilitarian thinkers are accused by their detractors of harboring a philosophy worthy only of pigs because it has no better or nobler pursuit than pleasure, and this seems "mean and groveling, as a doctrine worthy only of swine."[15] Mill answers this charge in the same way the ancient Epicureans answered it, namely, by saying that it is not utilitarians, but their critics, who are setting a "swinish" level for human beings because they assume that human beings are capable only of "swine-like" pleasures. In other words, people reject Epicureanism (often called ethical hedonism) or the greatest happiness principle because, in their minds, words like "pleasure" and "happiness" conjure images of profligacy, sensuality, and debauchery. If this is what "pleasure" means, then of course people reject it as an ethical guidepost. Mill, however, as did the Epicureans, rejects this criticism primarily because he views human beings as beings of higher capacity than animals and, thus, capable and more "fit" for higher pleasures. He explains:

The comparison of the Epicurean life to that of beasts is felt as degrading, precisely because a beast's pleasures do not satisfy a human being's conceptions of happiness. Human beings have faculties more elevated than the animal appetites and, when once made conscious of them, do not regard anything as happiness which does not include their gratification . . . [T]here is no known Epicurean theory of life which does not assign to the pleasures of the intellect, of the feelings and imagination, and of the moral sentiments a much higher value as pleasures than to those of mere sensation.[16]

So, here we see a strong distinction made between human and animal pleasures, and a statement of higher human faculties and capacities that inherently find pleasure in nobler things. Those nobler things fall in the realm of the mind, the emotions, and the conscience, rather than in the realm of the body or sensation. Mill is not denying humans the capacity for sensory or bodily pleasures, far from it. He is simply defending himself against the charge of expositing an ethos that places sensual pleasures as its cornerstone. Human beings, the only beings who have moral capacity and who develop moral philosophies, have higher capacities for pleasure than the animals and, thus, the pleasures set at the cornerstone of such a philosophy will be of a nobler nature.

Mill continues by saying that people who have ample experience in both higher and lower pleasures give a greater preference to the former type, and prefer a mode of existence that prioritizes higher pleasures. No person in their right mind, he claims, would trade places with an animal in exchange for the fullest measure of animal pleasures. The fullest animal pleasures, which are instinctual and bodily, do not compare to the higher human pleasures of the mind, the emotions, and the conscience, even if these higher pleasures are marked with some pain. Mill says:

A being of higher faculties requires more to make him happy, is capable probably of more acute suffering, and certainly accessible to it at more points, than one of an inferior type; but in spite of these liabilities, he can never really wish to sink into what he feels to be a lower grade of existence.[17]

Beings of higher capacity ultimately are not made truly happy by inferior pleasures. The happiness that is proper to human beings is one achieved not mainly in the domains of sensuality or corporeality, but primarily in the intellectual, emotional, and ethico-spiritual domains. This truth, according to Mill, is not undermined by the observed fact that people will often choose inferior pleasures at the expense of the higher. He acknowledges that people often choose against their better good in the name of a temporary, lesser pleasure. For example, some choose over-indulgence in food or drink at the expense of their health, which is the greater good and provides more enduring pleasure. Others will abandon higher pursuits for low-level selfishness and indolence. Mill explains this by reference to human character, saying that for whatever reasons people, at some point, lose touch with their inherent capacity for higher pleasures. He explains:

> Capacity for the nobler feelings is in most natures a very tender plant, easily killed, not only by hostile influences, but by mere want of sustenance; and in the majority of young persons it speedily dies away if the occupations to which their position in life has devoted them, and the society into which it has thrown them, are not favorable to keeping that higher capacity in exercise. Men lose their high aspirations as they lose their intellectual tastes because they have not time or opportunity for indulging them; and they addict themselves to inferior pleasure, not because they deliberately prefer them, but because they are either the only ones to which they have access or the only ones which they are any longer capable of enjoying.[18]

Mill the social theorist emerges in this passage. He spent much of his life writing about social reform and engaging in political activism to bring about positive changes in education, civic institutions, women's rights, and penal policy, many of which would find full endorsement by Gülen today. Moreover, the vast educational, cultural, and social activities of the Gülen movement would receive Mill's full endorsement as well. Mill's activism in all these areas is driven by his belief, which Gülen shares, in the inherent dignity of human beings, manifested here in the capacity for higher pleasures in the intellectual, emotional, and ethical domains. He firmly believed that all components of society should reflect this fact and should be ordered in such a way as to preserve and cultivate the capacities of inherent dignity in all people from the very earliest ages. Not to attempt to order society so is to commit a grave human and social injustice or, in Gülen's view perhaps, a sin.

Mill, in these passages, is defining pleasure in a specific way so as to distinguish it from the alleged pleasure of unbridled freedom in the merely sensual, corporeal realms. While a social principle of freedom he elaborates in *On Liberty* certainly gives people the room to waste their lives addicted to inferior pleasures at the expense of their highest and deepest selves, neither the principle nor his utilitarianism argues that such "freedom" is the highest goal of human life. One can argue, in fact, that that is not "freedom" at all, but instead is a specific form of slavery or addiction. Gülen can join the conversation here because throughout his work he draws a distinction between the life lived in search of the good, true, beautiful, and noble and the life wasted on the temporal, whimsical, and merely corporeal. We will discuss this distinction more in the next chapter, but for now let us say that Gülen defines freedom in a way parallel to Mill with regard to human dignity and capacity. Gülen says:

> Those who regard freedom as absolute liberty confuse human freedom with animal freedom. Animals have no moral questions asked of them and so are free of moral constraints. Some people desire this kind of freedom and, if they can, use it to indulge the darkest desires of the flesh. Such freedom is worse than bestial. True freedom, however, the freedom of moral responsibility, shows that one is human, for it motivates and enlivens the conscience and removes impediments to the spirit.[19]

Both Mill and Gülen, then, theorize human freedom in way that locates it within a larger philosophy of human flourishing. Neither of them views libertinism as the highest mark of freedom. On the contrary, both elaborate freedom as that which provides the ground for the fullest development and expression of the highest and best of human capacities, the fulfilment of which provides for people the most enduring pleasures. These pleasures are in the intellectual, spiritual, emotional, and ethical domains.

As I stated earlier, Gülen and Mill come from very different social, political, and religious contexts. No doubt, were they able to converse with each other face to face, they would differ in some of their determinations of the boundaries of freedom and tolerance in society. Both of them, however, agree on a point that is, in my view, much more fundamental to human life and flourishing, that is, freedom of thought and expression contextualized within a larger commitment to the general ideal of freedom. While people should be mindful of the possible consequences of their speech, they must still be able to think freely and express those thoughts in the world without fear of punishment. In my opinion, no direct and measurable harm is done to anyone from the simple expression in speech or writing of ideas. On the contrary, great health and benefit come to individuals and society as a whole when society structures itself to allow free thought, inquiry, and expression. Through this freedom human beings allow themselves the maximum room to develop their inherent capacities for conscience, imagination, emotion, spirituality, and intellect. Only when these are developed and given the room to develop by appropriate social and political structures do human beings thrive and reach the highest possible limits of their achievement.

Mill and Gülen are committed equally to this ideal of freedom within their respective contexts primarily because they are both humanists in the broadest sense of the term and the ideal of freedom is central to humanistic thinking. Moreover, as champions of human freedom, both are also champions of human greatness, not merely as an abstract ideal but as a necessary part of human collective life in the actual world. Gülen, like many others, has a clear vision of human greatness, of the traits that define great human beings, those who actualize in themselves the highest and best of human potential. It is to this vision of human greatness, the human ideal to be actualized in time and space, that we now turn.

3

Gülen, Confucius, and Plato
on the Human Ideal

The most expansive and systematic humanistic philosophies offer visions of a human ideal. In some cases, the ideal is social or collective in nature and includes politics, education, government, social structures, and so forth. In other instances, the vision focuses on the individual and how each person is to achieve the highest and best in human life. Examples of the former include the three most famous of the classical Greeks—Socrates, Plato, and Aristotle. The stoic writer Epictetus, the Epicureans, and the Buddha are examples of the latter. What emerges in almost of all these, however, is a vision of a human ideal as the goal for human development and achievement. Humanism, as it champions the human in these instances, holds forth an idealized, perfected form of it as a standard of measurement, as the goal to which all endeavor aspires, either for itself alone or for what it provides with regard to an ultimate, transcendent reality such as God.

In this chapter and the next, I construct a "trialogue" between Gülen and two of the most powerful expositors of the human ideal known to the world—Confucius and Plato. Interestingly, Confucius (551–479 BCE) and Plato (427–347 BCE) live within one generation or so of each other, one in China, the other in Athens, and articulate similar revolutionary visions of society and the individual based on what they believe about the inherent

possibilities of human nature, on the one hand, and the order or
"way" of things in larger reality, on the other. Gülen outlines a
vision of a spiritually renewed society whose strength and coherence come largely from the presence and efforts of people who have
perfected themselves, to the maximum extent possible, according to
the tenets of Islam. In the work of all three, Confucius, Plato, and
Gülen, we see a common claim that drives the whole of their respective visions: society works best when it is governed and constituted by people of moral and intellectual virtue. These people of
moral and intellectual virtue go by different names, of course, in
each thinker's work, and they exist within differing cultural, philosophical, and religious frameworks. They resonate, however, in
their deep essence, and it is this essence of the human ideal to
which we now turn.

Confucius, Plato, and Gülen, although coming from vastly different contexts and worldviews, share a fundamental view about
the structure of reality. All three articulate their respective visions of
human community with reference to a transcendent ideal that is the
basis, source, truth, or premise of all worldly reality. For Confucius,
this transcendent ideal is the *Dao*, or the Way of all things. The *Dao*
is not a god or personal deity; it is the natural force, principle, or
energy of Reality. All things exist in and of the *Dao*, in the Way of
all things. Both indigenous Chinese philosophies, Confucianism
and Daoism, posit the *Dao* as the deep grounding of all being,
essence, and reality, and only by flowing or integrating with, plug-
ging into, or imitating the *Dao* can harmony come to human life in
its social, political, and cosmic dimensions.

Plato describes this transcendent reality as the "ideal" over
against the "real" world. In the dialogues he constructs of his
teacher Socrates with his students, Socrates articulates these two
primary dimensions of existence, the ideal and the real, or sometimes in different terms, the Real and the shadow. The ideal or Real
is eternal, non-material, which means pure thought or spirit, immortal, unchanging, the source of Good, Truth and Justice, among other things. He symbolizes it with light or brightness, as opposed to

the shadowy darkness of empirical reality that human beings often mistake for true, ultimate reality. The real or shadow realm is material, changing, mortal, the realm of varying goods, competing truths, and relative notions of justice. In short, the ideal or Real world is the world of pure mind or spirit and its desires, while the real or shadow world is the world of the body and its desires. Human individual and collective life is good when the former governs the latter.

Finally, Gülen articulates his vision of human life within the framework of Islam, which posits a worldview similarly bifurcated between the earthly and the heavenly realms. Life on earth gains its fullness, meaning, and authenticity only when lived in cognizance of God, or *Allah*, as the true Source and grounding of all reality. In essence, all existent beings are Muslims, those in submission to God, because there is no existence at all outside the hand of God. When things go about their way fulfilling their lives and aims in the way of their inherent creation, they do so "in submission" to God, as Muslims. Specifically, life is most fully lived when consciously, not merely unconsciously, lived with a view toward the eternal Paradise of life in submission to God.

So, in all three instances, we see a version of a divided reality. Reality is one, to be sure, but comprised of different dimensions, realms, or ways of being. Those who know this and live mindfully of it find happiness, goodness, and truth, no matter their circumstances, because their orientation is ever upward toward higher reality. Those who live ignorant of this wallow in a swamp of confusion and corporeal lusts, blinded by finite, lower, "shadowy" reality. In short, there are two basic groups of people, the sighted and the blind; for life on earth to be good, it must be governed and guided by the former.

In *The Analects*, Confucius and others distinguish between those of "higher" or "noble" minds and those of "lower," "lesser" ways or "smaller" minds. Often, they are the mirror opposites of each other:

> A noble-minded person is different from others, but at peace with them. A small-minded person is the same as others, but never at peace with them.[1]

> The noble-minded encourage what is beautiful in people and dis-
> courage what is ugly in them. Little people do just the opposite.[2]

> The noble-minded seek within themselves. Little people seek
> elsewhere.[3]

In these passages, we see that noble-minded people possess an orientation categorically different from that of others. The noble-minded are people of larger capacity in all their inner dimensions, which allows them to be and act in the world in a way fundamentally different from others. The text continues:

> The noble-minded stand in awe of three things: the Mandate of
> Heaven, great men, and the words of a sage. Little people don't
> understand the Mandate of Heaven, so they aren't awed by it.
> They scorn great men, and they ridicule the words of a sage.[4]

> The noble-minded have nine states of mind: for eyes, bright;
> for ears, penetrating; for countenance, cordial; for demeanor,
> humble; for words, trustworthy; for service, reverent; for doubt,
> questioning; for anger, circumspect; and for facing a chance to
> profit, moral.[5]

The high-minded follow a different path in life from the low-minded. Theirs is an ear tuned to wisdom, discipline, dignity, and service, whereas common or "low" people possess no ear at all for such matters.

Plato articulates a similar division of people in *The Republic*, which is his longest dialogue. A great many works are devoted to interpretation of just this dialogue alone. I in no way intend an in-depth analysis of any part of the dialogue. Instead, I focus simply and exclusively on those passages that matter to us here. As indicated above, Plato divides reality into two realms, the eternal realm of pure thought or spirit and the finite realm of corporeality. Much of the conversation between Socrates and his students in the dialogue concerns the philosopher, or "lover of wisdom," who understands deeply this division in existence, and lives both from and toward the ideal, pure realm. Late in the dialogue, Socrates describes those who are not lovers of wisdom, do not understand True Reality, and therefore do not live or enjoy the benefits of a life lived attuned to wisdom. He says:

> So it is with those who have no experience with wisdom and virtue but constantly busy themselves instead with feasting and like activities. First, they seem to have been swept down to the bottom and then up again as far as the middle; then they roam and drift between the two points all their lives. Confined to these limits, they never look up to what is truly above them; nor have they been borne upward. Never have they been refreshed with reality's essence; never have they tasted pleasure that is pure and cannot deceive. Always they look down with their heads bent to the table. Like cattle, they graze, fatten, and copulate. Greed drives them to kick and butt one another with horns and hoofs of iron. Because they are insatiable, they slay one another. And they are insatiable because they neglect to seek real refreshment from that part of the soul that is real and pure. So they must live with the facades and illusions of true pleasure: their pleasures must be mixed with pain. It is this juxtaposition of sensations that gives to each its color and intensity, driving fools into frenzies of self-love. And all these deceptions are fought over in the same way that Stesichorus recounts the fighting at Troy for the ghost of Helen by men who didn't know the truth.[6]

As with Confucian teaching, the delineation is clear between the two groups of people: those who are wise and fix their attention on higher pleasures, and those who are ignorant and fix their attention on lower pleasures. At best, the common ignorant people raise their heads to a middle or medium point, but they spend most of their lives focused in a range between the middle and the low. As such, they are like grazing cattle, living a life focused on pleasures more suited to animals, which have no soul, than to humans, who possess an immortal soul.

Plato illustrates the distinction between philosophers and common people in Book 7 of *The Republic* with his famous allegory of the cave. Here, Socrates asks us to imagine people who have been living in a cave since childhood fixed in a position such that their gaze is locked onto the wall in front of them. What they do not see is that behind them stretches a long passage that leads out of the cave. Also behind them is a bright light shining in such a way that shadows of objects behind the people are cast onto the wall in front of them. The people live their lives facing the wall, engaging with the shadows on the wall as if they are true, real objects, not seeing that, in fact, they are only shadows, copies, or simulacra of the real objects. They hear echoes of sound in the cave and assume the sound comes from the shadows. They create stories about the shadows and give them meanings. The shadows are "reality" for the people.

But then, one of the people somehow breaks away from his fixed position and turns around to see the bright light shining, the shadows it creates, and the path leading upward out of the cave toward an even brighter light. He follows that path, his eyes hurting from the light, until he escapes the cave and emerges into the full light of day into the "real" world. He cannot see the full brightness of reality at first; his eyes must become accustomed to it through practice. Eventually, however, he sees clearly and fully and returns to the cave to tell the others of their darkness and of the light that can be theirs if they will but break free, turn away from the shadows, and follow the path to the light. They mock him, become angry with him and, eventually, plan to kill him for his ideas, which seem utterly ridiculous and out of touch with reality.[7]

The allegory is clear: A few people will craft their entire character toward the light of wisdom and truth and will give themselves to the pursuit of these despite the difficulties. Most, however, will prefer the cave of darkness and will spend their lives engaged with much easier "shadowy" pursuits at the expense of the higher pleasures more proper to beings who possess a soul. Socrates continues:

> We assert that this power is already in the soul of everyone. The way each of us learns compares with what happens to the eye: it cannot be turned away from darkness to face the light without turning the whole body. So it is with our capacity to know; together with the entire soul one must turn away from the world of transient things toward the world of perpetual being,

until finally one learns to endure the sight of its most radiant manifestation. This is what we call goodness, is it not?[8]

So, while the power to live life as a lover of wisdom lies in everyone, only some will actively live from this inner power. To do so involves turning one's entire orientation toward True Reality and resisting the allure of transient pleasures that, at best, are mere copies of the Truly Real. Again, for Plato as for Confucius, two basic kinds of people exist in the world, the sighted and the blind.

Gülen joins Plato and Confucius as he identifies the characteristics of ideal human beings which distinguish them from the common mass of humanity. People who exemplify the human ideal go by various names in Gülen's work, including "inheritors of the earth,"[9] "person of ideals,"[10] and "ideal people."[11] Whatever the moniker, they share distinct traits in common that sharply separate them from worldly people. In Gülen's view, renewal and renaissance will come to the world in general, and to Turkey specifically, when these ideal people raise themselves spiritually, morally, and intellectually to lead humanity, through their service and the example of their own lives, into a new era. Without such people, society continues in an unmanaged dance with all manner of opportunistic ideologies and sensualities, and the people inside such a society barely rise to the level of being called "human." Gülen says:

> Some live without thinking; some only think but cannot put their thoughts into practice . . . Those who live without thinking are the objects of the philosophy of others. Such persons always run from pattern to pattern, ceaselessly changing molds and forms, hectically struggling their whole life through, in deviations of thoughts and feelings, in personality disorders, and in metamorphoses of character and appearance, never being able to become their own selves . . . These people always resemble a pond of water which is infertile, barren, stagnant, and marred by a bad smell. Far from being able to express anything that is in the slightest way life-enhancing, it is inevitable that such people will become like a life-threatening bundle of viruses or a nest of microbes.[12]

These are Gülen's words, but they could be Plato's or Confucius' words just as easily. Here, Gülen does what his trialogue partners have done before him in delineating two types of people in the world, ideal people, or those who are conscious of and working toward the ideal, and worldly people. What worldly people have in common is that, on some level, they forget that they are people of value. Gülen continues:

> These people are so shallow in their thoughts and so superficial in their views that they imitate everything they hear or see, like children, drifting along behind the masses, hither and thither, never finding an opportunity to listen to themselves or be aware of or examine their worth; in fact, they never perceive that they have values peculiar to themselves. They live their lives as if they were slaves who can never accept freedom from their corporeal and bodily feelings . . . Consciously or unconsciously, they find themselves caught up in one or more such fatal nets every day and slaughter their souls over and over again in the most wretched of deaths.[13]

Like the inhabitants of Plato's cave, Gülen's worldly people live life fixed on finite, corporeal pleasures at the expense of higher pleasures of intellectual growth, spiritual development, and contribution to society. In doing so, they deny their humanity and live like animals. Gülen says with regard to the achievement of full humanity:

> Humans, however, are far from accomplishing such an achievement due to their corporeality and sensuality. Moreover, it can also be claimed that when humans are unaware of themselves or of their existence then they are lower than other creatures. Yet, humans, with their intellects, beliefs, consciences, and spirits are observers and commentators of the holy secrets that are found hidden between the lines of life. So, humans, no matter how insignificant they appear, are the "highest example," they are more beloved than all the others. Islam does not evaluate humankind without going to extremes. It is the only religion among all the belief systems which sees humans as being exalted creatures directed toward a special mission, equipped with superior potential and talents. According to Islam, humans are superior merely because they are human.[14]

Gülen's point is clear, even if some may question his claim of Islam's distinct view of the human. As discussed in the first chapter, Gülen argues for inherent human dignity and moral worth within the religio-philosophical system of Islam. Human beings who live unaware of, or in defiance of, this inherent value and promise are choosing a less-than-human life. Unfortunately, most people choose exactly this.

Yet, from among the masses arise a few extraordinary individuals who see past the transitory, conditional pleasures and pursuits of mundane life. These individuals, variously described by Confucius, Plato, and Gülen, achieve the human ideal and, as such, are the shining exemplars of what is possible in the realm of human life. For all three, hope for good human life on the individual and social or political levels rests with these people. All three, therefore, argue in their own way that these ideal individuals must take their place as leaders in society.

As indicated above, the Confucian superior man is distinguished from the masses by his moral character. Confucius and others in the tradition speak often of the central virtues that define the superior man and which actualize his deep humanity. These central virtues are commonly called the "constant virtues" of Confucianism. They vary in number as well as in "minor" or "major" designation depending on the commentator but nonetheless serve as a thorough collection of character traits that superior men exemplify. The virtues include: *ren*—humaneness, benevolence, goodness; *li*—ritual, etiquette, propriety; *yi*—righteousness, rightness; *zhi*—wisdom; *xin*—faithfulness, trustworthiness; *cheng*—sincerity; and *xiao*—filial piety. The tradition recounts Confucius emphasizing all these virtues and more. However, *ren* and *li* receive the most sustained treatment, and of these two, *ren* captures the essence of all virtue. *Ren* is the ground of all the virtues and, as commentator Laurence G. Thompson asserts, "Moral perfection was summed up in the term *ren* . . . [T]o Master K'ung it stood for such an exalted ideal that he had never known a person to whom the word could truly apply."[15] The focus on *ren* distinguishes Confucianism from forms of religion which propose an ideal rooted in social or political renunciation, asceticism, or the dietary, yogic, or alchemical practices common to other Chinese religious quests. The Literati Tradition, the name given to the Confucian tradition that calls for development of men superior in moral and intellectual virtue, emphasizes character building, regardless of blood lineage, which is then put into service of the state. *Ren* is the fullest moral ideal of goodness, humanity, and benevolence, and *ren* is cultivated in men by the *li*, the practice of ritual. A story from *The Analects* explains:

> Yen Hui asked about Humanity [*ren*], and the Master said: "Giving yourself over to Ritual [*li*]—that is Humanity. If a ruler gave himself to Ritual for even a single day, all beneath Heaven would return to Humanity. For doesn't the practice of Humanity find its source first in the self, and only then in others?"
> "Could you explain how giving yourself to Ritual works?" asked Yen Hui.
> "Never look without Ritual. Never listen without Ritual. Never speak without Ritual. Never move without Ritual."
> "I'm not terribly clever," said Yen Hui, "but I'll try to serve these words."[16]

The conviction here is that undying adherence to forms of propriety, etiquette, and ritual in every dimension of life demands a discipline that, in turn, one uses to cultivate in oneself a character of benevolence, goodness, and humanity. *Ren*, as a man develops it in himself, provides the grounding for him to develop all the other virtues through the constant practice of *li*. *Ren* here functions similarly to the good will in Kant's theory of moral character described in chapter 1. Without the good will, no other good is possible. Likewise, without *ren*, a basic inclination toward goodness and humanity, the other virtues have no basis.

As the superior man embodies the constant virtues and assumes his role in civil service, he comes to possess a power in society that is distinctly moral. The term for this is *te*, often translated as "moral force" or "integrity." The superior man's integrity civilizes and inspires those who surround him, such that his governance of them becomes an extension of his personal character. We read in *The Analects*:

> The Master said: "In government, the secret is Integrity [*te*]. Use it, and you'll be like the polestar: always dwelling in its proper place, the other stars turning reverently about it."[17]

> The Master said: "If you use government to show them the Way and punishment to keep them true, the people will grow evasive and lose all remorse. But if you use Integrity to show them the Way and Ritual to keep them true, they'll cultivate remorse and always see deeply into things."[18]

> Asking Confucius about governing, Lord Chi K'ang said: "What if I secure those who abide in the Way by killing those who ignore the Way, will that work?"
> "How can you govern by killing?" replied Confucius. "Just set your heart on what is virtuous and benevolent, and the people will be virtuous and benevolent. The noble-minded have the Integrity [*te*] of wind, and little people the Integrity of grass. When the wind sweeps over grass, it bends."[19]

> The Master wanted to go live among the nine wild tribes in the east. Someone asked: "How could you bear such vulgarity?"
> "If someone noble-minded live there," replied the Master, "how could vulgarity be a problem?"[20]

The contention in these passages is that *te* is a force in and of itself, enough to govern the behavior of others when manifested in the life of a superior man. A superior man exhibiting *te* consistently has little or no trouble governing the people of a society because they are inspired by his good example to the point of even having virtuous qualities come out in them by his example. Because of his virtue, they feel remorse over their immorality. Because of his virtue, they will follow his guidance in virtuous ways despite themselves. Because of his virtue, they will reform their vulgar ways and he will not have to force them to do so. Inherent in these claims is the Confucian belief in a basic human nature that is inherently good. Confucius is not naïve about human beings and their possibilities for evil; he sees this clearly enough. Instead, he remains convinced that morally good human nature can be cultivated with deliberate, devoted practice because of its inherent qualities that make it receptive to such cultivation. Moreover, this receptivity means that human nature responds to demonstrations of moral goodness by reforming itself, in however small ways, in the direction of that moral goodness. Thus, the grass bends with the wind, and the lesser stars turn around the polestar. Such is the power of *te*.

Confucius argues consistently throughout the tradition that without the services of superior men, these paragons of moral and intellectual virtue, society descends into chaos. Society falls victim to rank materialism, empty ritual, small-mindedness, and moral turpitude. Indeed, this is how Confucius assessed the society of his day, and his teachings are meant to address this grave problem. For him, in society there can be no order or harmony that does not begin with the internal character of moral individuals who then contribute their moral virtue to society through government service. Thus, Confucianism is as much a political theory as it is a moral or religious theory. Moreover, it is a humanistic or naturalistic theory that prioritizes individuals who commit themselves to actualizing in their own person the highest possible human achievement, the ideal of moral and intellectual perfection.

Like Confucius, Plato provides a theory of moral development and political governance in *The Republic* that centers on the existence of an ideal human who is a lover of wisdom, or a "philosopher." Plato's dialogues feature his revered teacher Socrates as the chief example of such a philosopher in every respect. Socrates, thus, embodies the human ideal as he appears in Plato's dialogues, and he teaches the ideal to the young men who gather around him. Both his life and his ideas instruct his students, those who sat with him in ancient Athens, and those who read Plato's dialogues today.

The Socratic "persona" is well defined throughout Plato's dialogues, but perhaps the *Apology*, *Crito*, and *Phaedo* illustrate this persona most dramatically. Socrates, in these dialogues, confronts the Athenian jury that has charged and eventually convicts him of impiety and of corrupting the youth of the city. He then submits to the imposed death sentence and, in the famous final lines of *Phaedo,* drinks the poisonous hemlock given him by the guard and dies. Socrates, as he defends himself against the charges before the jury, articulates his vision of the ideal human life; that is, he describes the highest and best kind of life to live and defends himself as having lived trying to understand and achieve this life for himself and others. He continues explaining and exemplifying this highest and best life in *Crito* and *Phaedo* as he lives out his last days in jail and is visited by his students.

Chief among the philosopher's traits, as taught and exemplified by Socrates, is wisdom. The word "philosopher," of course, means "lover of wisdom." This is explained, however, quite paradoxically in the *Apology*. As it turns out, the philosopher is wise because he admits that he knows very little or nothing. Socrates is the wisest man because he knows, unlike the professional tutors and Sophists of his day, that he is not wise. Wisdom is precisely this, knowing the limitations of human knowledge, especially when the process of learning is arrested through arrogance or apathy. The result of this special kind of wisdom is a life lived precisely to acquire knowledge, to seek it out wherever and however possible. In short, Socrates lived and proposed that others live a life in pursuit of truth, and a life in pursuit of truth examines everything over and over again. Therefore, the image Plato presents of his teacher in all the dialogues is of a man who is willing to forsake all other pursuits in exchange for an in-depth conversation and inquiry into the nature of worthy things: love, beauty, goodness, justice, and so on. Socrates never tires of such conversations, even when he has what appear to be settled or firm convictions about these matters. He is always willing to inquire further, to prolong examination, to test even firm conclusions. Such a life posture generates what is one of the most famous of Socrates' sayings: "The unexamined life is not worth living."[21]

Socrates embodies other characteristics of the human ideal, or philosopher, including caring for the soul more than the body, fearing wickedness more than death, and being impervious to the opinions of the masses. This last topic is important for our discussion here. Socrates tells Crito that he should live his life seeking the opinions only of the good and knowledgeable, not of the masses. The masses are given to myriad opinions about everything and tend to focus on immediate, material gain at the expense of eternal realities. Therefore, Crito should seek the opinions and approval only of the wise few. At the heart of all these statements is a deep moral conviction that the highest and best human life is a life of cultivated virtue or excellence. Moreover, as Socrates explains in *The Republic*, those individuals who possess such virtue must be placed in charge of the state; otherwise, disorder and tyranny are inevitable.

The idea that order comes to life when virtue rules is a consistent theme in Socrates' teaching, and it is the central theme of *The Republic*. He argues that the virtuous "part" of an entity must govern all other parts in order for orderliness, harmony, and goodness to exist in the whole of the entity. This is true both at the individual and the collective levels. Individuals' lives run properly when they govern from the highest and best part of themselves, their soul, which is inherently attuned to the highest virtues of goodness, truth, and justice. Likewise, a society finds order, harmony, and justice when the highest and best members of the society govern all the rest. These highest and best are the philosophers, the morally cultivated individuals discussed above, whom he identifies later as the "guardians" of the state. Socrates admits that some may find incredible the idea that philosophers must be kings, but he nevertheless insists upon it. He speaks to Glaucon, one of the young men with him:

> Unless philosophers become kings in our cities, or unless those who now are kings and rulers become true philosophers, so that political power and philosophic intelligence converge, and unless those lesser natures who run after one without the other are excluded from governing, I believe there can be no end to troubles, my dear Glaucon, in our cities or for all mankind. Only then will our theory of the state spring to life and see the

light of day, at least to the degree possible. Now you see why I held back so long from speaking out about so troublesome a proposition. For, it points to a vexing lesson: whether in private or public life there is no other way to achieve happiness.[22]

Important to note in this passage is Socrates' identification as of "lesser nature" those who seek either political power or philosophical intelligence alone, and not in combination with the other. His contention here is that the former without the latter results in tyranny and corruption, whereas the latter without the former results in triviality and uselessness. Those with political power but without the true philosophical intelligence to use it will govern the state with a view toward personal gain and exploitative power. Those with philosophical intelligence but with no view toward political application of their knowledge will waste their energies on intellectual whims and trifles that have no useful application. Therefore, these two domains must be combined and true philosophers must be rulers.

True philosophers, of course, are those described earlier, those who care more for eternal rather than temporal realities, who seek the light rather than the darkness of the cave, who live like the immortal souls they are, rather than as the eating and copulating animals most people choose to emulate. Only such individuals, men and women who live in common with no concern for personal, private wealth even at the level of personal family life, can guide the ship of state so that goodness, order, and truth prevail in all its workings.* These true philosophers seek the truth above all else, and seek it in order to live by it individually and collectively. No possibility for social and political harmony exists outside their governance.

Socrates admits that his republican ideal may never be accomplished fully in reality, yet he nevertheless insists that those who care for society must try to achieve it as much as is possible. Otherwise, only anarchy and tyranny remain as the eventual options for society. Both Confucius and Socrates see clearly in their lifetimes the

---

* Socrates asserts elsewhere in *The Republic* that, in addition to being philosophers, the guardians can be either male or female, and they must not own private property but must hold it all in common, including children.

depths to which society can sink when those with no concern for goodness or truth control the levers of power. The chaotic possibilities present in antiquity remain alive today in the contemporary world and, thus, Gülen today articulates a vision for the guidance of society largely resonant with those of his ancient colleagues. For Gülen, as for Confucius and Socrates, hope for society lies exclusively in the influence of the "ideal humans."

Gülen's reflections on the world of Islam and particularly on Anatolian history and destiny parallel Confucius' reflections on ancient China. Both men refer to a past period of greatness that has been lost and that now must be regained. Confucius regularly refers to ancient governors, emperors, and others from past generations as examples of nobility and wisdom that must now, in his time, be emulated if China is to restore itself to its former greatness and avoid fragmentation and tyranny. Gülen, too, reflects on the glorious past of the Ottoman Empire, a time when Turkish civilization was at its peak, and when Islam as both a religion and as a culture attained global supremacy in significant measure. In his assessment, the true greatness of the Ottomans was found in their commitment to high ideals that sought the good for the society of the time as well as for the future, and in their Islamic essence to the extent that they emulated the four caliphs of early Islam after the death of the Prophet Muhammad. Gülen claims that while notable figures like the Pharaohs, Caesar, and Napoleon are infamous for their actions, their works have no enduring nature because they were motivated in their essence not by high ideals for all of humanity and for the future, but by personal ambition, greed, and lust for power. Gülen says of them:

> [T]heir noisy and hectic lives, which bedazzled so many, never became, and can never become, promising for the future in any way. For those people were the poor, the wretched, who subjugated truth to the command of might, who always sought social ties and congruity around self-interest and profit, and who live their lives as slaves, never accepting freedom from spite, selfishness, and sensuality.[23]

The lack of high ideals and eternal values for the present and the future prevents the work of these memorable figures from having any lasting, positive influence. Such is not the case, however, for the caliphs and the Ottomans, according to Gülen. He says:

> In contrast, first the Four Rightly-Guided Caliphs and later the Ottomans presented such great works, whose consequences exceed this world and reach to the next, that these works are in essence able to compete with the centuries; of course, only for those who are not beguiled by temporary eclipses. Although they lived their lives and duties fully and passed away, they will always be remembered, talked of, and find a place in our hearts as the good and the admirable. In every corner of our country, the spirit and essence of such people as Alparslan, Melikşah, Osman Gazi, Fatih, and many others, waft like the scent of incense, and hopes and glad tidings flow into our spirits from their vision.[24]

A qualitative difference exists for Gülen between figures like Caesar, Napoleon, and the Pharaohs, on the one hand, and Fatih, Süleyman the Magnificent, and the Four Caliphs, on the other. The difference lies in their respective embodiment of, or submission to, high ideals of goodness, truth, morality, and justice. Such ideals are the only legitimate basis of a social, political, or cultural agenda that will produce good for its own time and for the future. Gülen sees a reclaiming of these ideals in contemporary Turkey, as a new generation of people committed to high ideals comes into fruition. He says, "there are now, in huge numbers, lofty representatives— or candidates soon-to-be—of science, knowledge, art, morality, and virtue who are inheritors of all the values of our glorious past."[25]

Gülen describes his ideal humans extensively throughout his work, but perhaps nowhere more succinctly than in *The Statue of Our Souls*. In this work, he uses the terms "person of ideals" or "inheritors of the earth" to refer to the intellectually and morally virtuous people who actualize true humanity and, thus, must lead society in order for it to be good. In fact, as Gülen exposits it, the idea here is of a people and the spiritual culture they embody that come to have prominence in earthly life because of their righteous-ness. God gives them this prominence as a gift and it is theirs as a responsibility and duty until their own unworthiness demands that God take it from them. Gülen quotes a passage from the Qur'an, which in turn refers to the Torah, in which God says "My Servants, the righteous, shall inherit the earth."[26] Gülen goes on to say:

> Without doubt that promise, guaranteed in this verse by an oath, will be fulfilled one day. Nor, without doubt, is it the inheritance of the Earth only; for inheriting the Earth also means governing and managing the resources of the sky and space. It will be almost a universal "dominion." As this domin-ion is one that will be deputed to a regent or steward on behalf of the Lord, it is extremely important, indeed essential, that the attributes that are appropriate to inheriting the Earth and the heavens are conformed to. Indeed, only so far as the required attributes are realized and practiced can the dream come true.[27]

Gülen continues by explaining that in past eras Islamic civiliza-tion held the title of "inheritor of the earth," but lost that place because of failures in both internal and external dimensions, that is, in the inner realm of heart and soul, and in the outer realm of con-temporary knowledge. Muslim societies lost their way spiritually and intellectually and, thus, lost their place as "inheritors of the earth," which then came to be held by other entities in the West. Throughout his work, Gülen consistently calls for the revival of Islam in spiritual and intellectual terms, for it to restore itself to itself, so that all humanity and the earth itself will come into a glo-rious new age of tolerance and peace. Through a cadre of highly vir-tuous individuals, Islam and, Gülen hopes, Turkey, can be restored to a position of global prominence to lead the world into that new age.

Important to note here is that Gülen nowhere in his work calls for any kind of political or governmental activity to bring about this new era. Gülen is not a politician, or a political theorist, and he is not, unlike Confucius and Plato, calling for a new generation of political leaders. This is a central difference between Gülen and his trialogue partners in this chapter and the next. Gülen's ideas, which are iterations of larger Islamic ideals, do not rely on governmental power for their implementation. On the contrary, Gülen focuses on the re-establishment of a cultural, intellectual, and humanitarian understanding that comes through common people of virtue and service living out their lives in their various professional, community, and familial roles. The "dominion" Gülen refers to here is not a dominion of elite political leaders over all others; rather, it is the dominion and pre-eminence of a worldview characterized by peace, knowledge, spirituality, tolerance, and love. Moreover, this worldview comes to prominence because of the myriad of people who, through their virtue and stewardship, come to qualify as inheritors of the earth.

Gülen spends an entire chapter in *The Statue of Our Souls* enumerating the traits of the inheritors of the earth, and it is in this enumeration that we see Gülen's most succinct articulation of the human ideal as he envisions it within an Islamic perspective. He identifies eight central attributes of the inheritors of the earth,[28] or as he calls them elsewhere, the "people of ideals." These traits are perfect faith, love, scientific thinking passed through the prism of Islam, self-assessment and criticism of viewpoints and perspectives, free thinking and respect for freedom of thought, social conscience and a preference for consultative decision-making, mathematical thinking, and artistic sensitivity.

This list seems, on its surface, to be quite different from the list of virtues of the Confucian superior man, or from Socrates' virtues, but closer inspection reveals strong parallels between all three. Perfect faith and love, for Gülen's person of ideals, is rooted within an Islamic perspective firmly grounded in submission to God. The faith and love here listed are contextualized within that larger frame of eternal reference that submission to God provides. This faith and love will not be misplaced onto or seek final fruition in worldly or material things and thus lead all civilization down a path of rank materialism and sensuality. It keeps its eyes fixed on eternal realities, in the same way Socrates' guardians do. The scientific and mathematical thinking of Gülen's inheritors of the earth is a perspective rooted in the conviction that Truth is One, that it is not divided into disparate categories of religious truth versus scientific truths, or the truths of faith versus the truths of reason. Truth is indivisible for inheritors of the earth and they seek to understand all truth with the rigor of science and mathematics, eager to advance scientific understanding of the cosmos as an infinitely intricate "holy book" of the workings of the Creator. Like Confucian superior men, they excel in many disciplines of knowledge, not only in "religious" knowledge. In matters of governance and decision-making, the inheritors of the earth act with a view toward the good of the community, not merely personal good. Moreover, they value consultation and dialogue as the best route to good decision-making. Like Socrates' guardian class, they submit themselves to each other's questioning and analysis in order to emerge with a consensus that is good for everyone. Like both Socrates' guardians and Confucian superior men, the inheritors of the earth are hard on themselves in that they hold themselves up to intense scrutiny, challenging their own ideas and perspectives, ever purifying and refining themselves and their ideas in their thirst for truth and virtue. Finally, like the guardians and the superior men, the inheritors of the earth value beauty wherever it is found, and they know that only in the free exercise of thought and creativity can cultivated souls create new visions of the world and humanity, be it in the domains of aesthetics, philosophy, governance, or elsewhere.

The central difference between Gülen's inheritors of the earth and the Confucian superior men or the Socratic guardians is that the former are Muslims, and generate their entire being and worldview from within an Islamic perspective. What keeps the rule of the Muslim inheritors of the earth from being an oppressive tyranny is exactly what prevents the rule of Socrates' guardians or Confucian superior men from being a tyranny, namely, a concern for the good of all humanity and a fundamental acknowledgement of the inherent value of all human beings because of their likeness to the divine, as discussed in chapter 1. Gülen describes these inheritors of the earth at great length. He says:

A person of such character will always run from victory to victory. Not, however, in order to ruin countries and set up capitals on the ruins, but rather to move and activate humane thoughts, feelings, and faculties, to strengthen us with so much love, affection, and benevolence that we will be able to embrace everything and everybody, to restore and repair ruined sites, to blow life into the dead sections of society, to become the blood and life and thus flow within the veins of beings and existence and to make us feel the vast pleasures of existence. With all that such a person has, they are a man of God and as His vicegerent they are always in contact with the creation. All their acts and attitudes are controlled and supervised. Everything they do, they do as if it were to be presented for His inspection; they feel by what He feels; they see by His look; they derive their way of speech from His Revelation; they are like the dead man in the hands of the *ghassal** before His Will; their greatest source of power is their awareness of their own weakness, inability, and poverty before Him, and they always try to do their utmost, and not to make a mistake in order to make the best use of that endless treasure.[29]

Gülen's inheritors of the earth, clearly, are not conquerors in the name of God or Islam. They are not *jihadists* waging war against the infidel. Instead, they are people of incredible virtue, goodness, and love who give themselves wholly to the highest ideals and seek to create a world in which all people have the opportunity to actualize their fullest human potential in every domain of life, from the most mundane to the most transcendent. Moreover, it is a world in which the community members themselves provide an inspirational example of that fully actualized humanity.

These people of ideals are central to any workable, good, and enduring society. Without them, both the ideals and the people who embody them, a society's legacy is muted, at best, and the good that it appears to achieve is ephemeral or short-lived. Gülen says:

If the officials running a good and virtuous state are chosen because of their nobility in spirit, ideals, and feelings, the state

---

* The person who conducts the ritual bath for the dead in Islam.

> will be good and strong. A government run by officials who
> lack these high qualities is still a government, but it is neither
> good nor long-lasting. Sooner or later, its officials' bad behav-
> ior will appear as dark spots on its face and blacken it in the
> people's eyes.[30]

> Power's dominance is transitory; while truth's and justice's
> dominance is eternal. Even if these do not exist today, they will
> be victorious in the very near future. For this reason, sincere
> politicians should align themselves and their policies with truth
> and justice.[31]

Gülen, like his trialogue partners, insists that society's goodness
directly depends upon the goodness of those who lead it; moreover,
the leaders and the other community members who embody these
traits sacrifice all personal ambition to the good of the whole. They
give their whole selves in service to humankind, never ceasing to
think of the future. They ground themselves in eternal spiritual values, and they assess the merit of all scientific and technological
gains with a view toward these eternal values. Gülen says of them:

> They will be completely truth-loving and trustworthy and, in
> support of truth everywhere, always ready to leave their fami-
> lies and homes when necessary. Having no attachment to
> worldly things, comforts, or luxuries, they will use their God-
> given talents to benefit humanity and plant the seeds of a happy
> future. Then, constantly seeking help and success from God,
> they will do their best to protect those seeds from harm, just as
> a hen protects its eggs. Their entire lives will be dedicated to
> this way of truth . . . These new people will unite profound
> spirituality, diverse knowledge, sound thinking, a scientific
> temperament, and wise activism. Never content with what they
> know, they will continuously increase in knowledge: knowl-
> edge of self, of nature, and of God.[32]

Gülen here describes the ideal people as those who escape the
perennial temptations Socrates mentions in *The Republic*, namely,
the temptations of attachment to worldly pleasures, wealth, and private comforts. Gülen's ideal people, like Socrates' guardians, do not
succumb to such temptations because their natures are constructed

so as always to seek eternal pleasures and truths, at the expense of the temporal. Also, like Socrates and the guardians, they are never content with themselves and their knowledge. They always push further and higher, hungry for new heights of knowledge, virtue, goodness, and truth. For Gülen, only when Turkish society, and all societies, are made up of or influenced by such individuals will human civilization then be turned toward life, vitality, and health instead of death and decay.

Again, Gülen's vision for leadership is expansive, and it functions in a distinctly apolitical way. His sermons and teachings do not comprise, in themselves, a system of governance or political theory, as do Confucius' teachings and Plato's ideas in *The Republic*. Gülen is a Muslim preacher and theologian, not a political scientist or activist. He does not call his listeners specifically to run for office or to take over the commands of government. He does not call for the dissolution of current systems of governance. While his vision for society certainly includes ideal people holding positions of authority in government, he mostly does not speak in such specific terms. Instead, Gülen speaks of a community leadership dispersed throughout society in the myriad professions. People of ideals will shape society as they give themselves fully to their respective endeavors as scientists, teachers, business people, service workers, parents, public servants, laborers, and the like. The image is more of a mass, grassroots movement of people who then choose, via democratic process, people who embody virtuous ideals to serve and guide the state. The end result, however, is the same for Confucius, Plato, and Gülen: the existence of a stable, good society that exists as such for its citizens because it is run by people who actualize in themselves the highest possible human ideals of virtue and goodness.

So, all three of our trialogue participants, from within their own distinct worldviews and historical eras, have crystallized for us a central feature of what is required to live a good human life at the individual and collective level. That central feature is virtue, both intellectual and moral. People will live the fullest, and therefore the happiest, of human lives when they set their sights on developing themselves into people of intellectual and moral virtue. Moreover, society as a whole achieves its highest and most beneficial development when it is guided by those individuals of high moral and intellectual virtue, who are those best able to see the good for all, instead of merely the good for the privileged few or for themselves alone. These virtuous people will guide society such that all its members will have ample opportunities to develop themselves to the fullest human capacity they can.

The question now becomes: From where do these people of virtue come? Where are we to find these people of high character and leadership who will guide our social and collective existence toward goodness, truth, and justice? Do these people come down to us from the heavens fully formed and ready to rule? Are they divine beings who walk among us? No, these people are entirely people, not divine beings, they are born to human mothers and fathers, and they must be raised and educated to be the paragons of virtue that society requires for its fullest existence. All three of our trialogue participants agree that education is the means by which we as a society of people develop from among ourselves these virtuous individuals. So, it is to their respective theories of education that we now turn in the next chapter.

4

Gülen, Confucius, and Plato on Education

The last chapter ended with a question about the origin of the superior men, the philosopher-kings, or the inheritors of the earth. These are the monikers Confucius, Plato, and Gülen respectively give to their versions of the ideal human who is to lead or influence society if, as a whole, it is to be good and just. Where are these people? How do we get them? Where do we find them? The answer, of course, is obvious if not comforting. We are them, or we are to become them. The goal of all three systems is for all people to actualize the human ideal in themselves as much as possible. The phrase "as much as possible," however, acknowledges that many people, even most perhaps, will not achieve this high level of human possibility. As we saw early in the last chapter, Confucius, Plato, and Gülen all mark clearly the distinction between the sighted and the blind, between the masses of common people fixated on mundane realities and the few who seek after higher things. So, while all have the potential to become ideal people because of their inherent human nature, most will not, or will only in partial or piecemeal ways.

For those who do come to actualize the human ideal, the question still remains: How did they do it? What methods or mechanisms put them in a position to cultivate themselves to such a degree? The answer is the same from all three of our trialogue participants:

through education. Education is the general ground upon which rests any effort to actualize full or ideal humanity. Confucius, Plato, and Gülen each articulate specific theories of education in their respective worldviews, so much so that without the education component, the entire edifice of the system falls. Moreover, each of them articulates a specific kind of education that will bring about or maximize the highest possibility of attaining the kind of human cultivation of character that each of them seeks. In short, for Confucius, Plato, and Gülen, rigorous and guided education is the cornerstone of development of the highest human ideal; therefore, social structures must be ordered fundamentally around the mechanisms of this education in order for society to generate from within itself its own highest and best leaders.

As we saw in the previous chapter, Confucianism exists as a socio-political theory as much or more than as a religious philosophy. As he articulates the distinction between the masses, on the one hand, and the "superior man" or "gentleman," on the other, Confucius advances his view that harmony in human social and political life occurs when superior men govern. Following this claim, Confucianism exists through the centuries in China as a philosophical theory of social and political development that educates men to prepare them for varying levels of government service, all the way to being principal advisors to the Emperor. Confucius, however, concerned himself with people as a whole, not only with would-be rulers, and with society as a whole. David Hinton, in the introduction to his translation of *The Analects*, explains that for Confucius ritual involved far more than simply saying the proper words to an elder, or wearing the proper color during a festival season. Ritual involves one's proper posture inside a web of relationships that comprise human life—relationships with parents, siblings, older relatives, imperial authorities, venerable historical texts, and so on. Living a life of *li*, or ritual propriety, in this sense naturally involves a broad set of egalitarian principles with which Confucius primarily was concerned, principles like social justice, governance in accord with what is good for society (not for the rulers alone), and the role intellectuals play in guiding society and critiquing its governors. Hinton says:

> For Confucius, the Ritual community depends upon these egalitarian elements, and they depend ultimately on the education and cultivation of the community members. To call Confucius' contribution in this regard epochal would be an understatement. He was China's first professional teacher, founding the idea of a broad moral education, and in addition, he established the classic texts that defined the essential content of that education. As if that weren't enough, he also established the enduring principle of egalitarian education—that all people should receive some form of education, that this is necessary for the health of a moral community. He focused his attention on the education of the intellectuals, which was of necessity much more exhaustive than that of the masses, but he thought even this education should be available to any who seek it, however humble their origins. In fact, not only was the Master himself from a relatively humble background, nearly all his disciples were as well.[1]

The Confucian commitment to education is, in fact, a commitment to the human, to human beings in themselves and in community, and to humaneness as the chief moral virtue that both defines what it means to be a human being and anchors a good, stable society. Without this basic development, society simply does not work because the people who comprise it function barely at the level called "human."

Commentators both inside and outside the Chinese tradition routinely refer to Confucian superior men as "scholars" because of the exacting educational regimen the men had to master in order to achieve any rank at all in civil service. Moreover, for Confucius, learning is central to all virtue. *The Analects* tell us:

> The Master asked: "Have you heard of the six precepts and their six deceptions?" "No," replied Adept Lu. "Then sit, and I'll tell you," said the Master. "To love Humanity without loving learning: that's the deception of foolishness. To love wisdom without loving learning: that's the deception of dissipation. To love

sincerity without loving learning: that's the deception of sub-terfuge. To love veracity without loving learning: that the deception of intolerance. To love courage without loving learn-ing: that's the deception of confusion. And to love determina-tion without loving learning: that's the deception of reckless-ness."[2]

Here, Confucius explains that to strive to actualize any of the virtues of life and service without learning is a variety of deception. The virtues somehow do not become virtuous without being accompanied by, or acquired through, education or learning. Elsewhere in *The Analects*, Confucius says "I've spent days without food and nights without sleep, hoping to purify thought and clar-ify mind. But it's never done much good. Such practices—they're nothing like devoted study."[3] Devoted study and learning develop the moral virtues of cleanliness of heart and mind. Traditional asce-tic practices such as fasting or sleep deprivation are ineffective.

Confucian "superior men" or "gentlemen" were master students and practitioners of what later came to be called the Confucian Classics, or the Canon of the Literati. The texts included in the canon expanded over time, but the oldest, most venerable portion of the canon which often bears the title of "scripture" includes five texts: *Shu Ching* (Book of History); *Shih Ching* (Book of Songs); *Yi Ching* (Book of Changes); *Ch'un-Ch'iu* (Springs and Autumns); and *Li Ching* (Book of Ritual).[4] Confucian superior men were schol-ars whose mastery of the content of these texts and others qualified them as worthy to serve as government officials, provincial gover-nors, and imperial advisors. The various texts of the Confucian canon provide extensive instruction on the cultivation of character aligned with the classic virtues of humaneness, propriety, prudence, uprightness, incorruptibility, frugality, filial piety, benevolence, dis-cipline, and sincerity. Additionally, they taught excellence in music, poetry, and other knowledge. In *The Analects*, we read:

> The Master said: "How is it, my little ones, that none of you study the *Songs*? Through the *Songs*, you can inspire people to turn their gaze inward, bring people together and give voices to their grievances. Through them you serve your father when

home and your sovereign when away, and you learn the names of countless birds and animals and plants." Then the Master said to his son, Po-yu: "Have you worked through the *Chou Nan* and the *Shao Nan?** Until you've worked through at least them, you'll live as if you stood facing a wall."[5]

Here, we see that mastery of the Book of Songs, that is, music and poetry, is vital to self-development, leadership, and service of both family and emperor. Without this cultivation, life is like "facing a wall." The resonance with Plato's allegory of the cave is obvious here. Without mastery of at least the first sections of the Book of Songs, the would-be superior man is like one of Plato's cavedwellers, fixed in position staring at the wall of shadows as if it is the culmination of all reality. Only through study is one able to turn away from the wall and go toward the light of knowledge; only those with knowledge can fulfill society's need for strong families, good governors, and a wisely advised emperor. Without these things, society devolves into chaos.

The educational path through the Classics cultivated a mastery of more than merely the art or science of governing. Confucian education was not so narrowly defined. As indicated by even the titles of the Classics themselves, Confucian scholars were trained in a variety of disciplines, such as poetry, music, history, and ritual, which on the surface might not seem integral to education in good governance. Scholars were master musicians on a variety of instruments, excelled in poetry composition and recitation, and were highly skilled calligraphers, just to list a few areas of expertise. The Confucian theory argues that such education and training cultivates character in a complex and desirable way. We see a hint of this in a passage from *The Analects*:

> The Master said: "When I keep saying *Ritual! Ritual!*, do you think I'm just ranting about jade and silk? And when I keep saying *Music! Music!*, do you think I'm just ranting about bells and drums?"[6]

---

* The first two chapters in the Book of Songs.

The implication here is that more is being taught than simply the mechanics of ritual or music. Certainly, ritual and music have inherent value that alone would encourage study and mastery of them, but Confucius suggests here that mastery of these accomplishes something else as well, beyond the level of propriety in dress or the playing of instruments. The passage quoted earlier about the Book of Songs contains a similar suggestion, namely, that learning music provides an education beyond the mere performance of songs, or the history of musical tradition.

Here, we get a glimpse of what Confucius claims about human nature and its depths. Mastery in music, poetry, and ritual provides a mechanical mastery of instruments, words, and actions, to be sure, which is useful on its own. At a deeper level, however, mastery in these subjects cultivates a humaneness of character that is of the greatest importance. Music opens up a part of the human spirit that nothing else can; to be able to both play and hear music at a high level demands the fine, exquisite cultivation of that innermost part of human nature. The same applies to poetry or calligraphy. Both demand increasingly subtle and fine powers of perception and expression, at the level of the mechanics of the hand or speaking voice, and at the level of the soul.*

This is the point for Confucius. Superior men become superior human beings through the cultivation of this ever more pristine capacity within themselves, a capacity which they share with all human beings, but which they alone through their education and discipline, actualize in themselves. As they develop themselves in these areas, their influence on others grows because all human beings, cultivated or not, possess a nature that responds to music and other beauty. As the passage above indicates, music prompts people to look inside themselves, to come together with others, and to express their feelings. Scholars with musical mastery inspire these in people;

---

* Space in this chapter does not permit what would be an interesting comparison between the artistic achievements of Confucian scholars and those of Islamic calligraphers, both of which derive from their respective philosophical or religious perspectives.

this inspirational power comprises part of their *te* discussed in the previous chapter.

Confucian superior men exemplified the human intellectual and moral ideal of Chinese thought for centuries, even until Chairman Mao and communism. These masters of literary education and moral development defined true humanity in its most august, exalted form, and the image that emerges of them is of one of high intellectual and artistic refinement, thorough cultivation of personality, exquisite propriety and form, and supreme moral elegance. Moreover, they achieved this through devoted study and tireless practice, that is, on their own strength. Many humanistic systems prioritize, as this one does, what human beings can accomplish through their own efforts, as opposed to assistance from God or fate. Confucius tells us that basic human nature is the same in everyone; what distinguishes people eventually is study and practice which they do on their own through their own determination. Such people are the rightful owners of the title "superior men," and others who do not achieve such distinction should be grateful to be governed by them and to have them as examples of proper human life and behavior. Indeed, according to Confucius, a superior man's character exerts a kind of moral force on those around him such that they feel themselves wanting to do noble actions, or at least refrain from base ones. These are people who not only enhance their own individual lives, they enhance life itself for all those near them through their example and their governance. As the ideal human actualized in social and political life, they testify to the power of education and cultivation in human life.

Confucian superior men, were they to be transported across time and space to Plato's ideal republic, would find themselves welcomed and encouraged to take their place among the guardians. As we saw in the previous chapter, both versions of the idealized human being involve high moral development and a component of service to society through governance. What also unites them is the belief that only those proven fit to govern should actually govern. Therefore, the political model proposed by both philosophies is a meritocracy, as opposed to a pure blood aristocracy. Those with merit should govern, and those without merit must be governed, or helped to govern themselves. Merit is determined through the educational system, so the path to guardianship in Plato's ideal republic, as in the Confucian path to government service, requires substantial formal education and cultivation.

Socrates' ideas about education for the guardians, as well as for all other roles in a well-ordered society, are spread throughout the entirety of *The Republic*. Books 2 and 3 provide substantial conversations about specific components of educational curricula. Later books delve into the moral benefits of mathematical education, and even later sections explain Socrates' notion of the meritocracy by contrasting it with four aberrant forms of government, namely, timocracy, oligarchy, radical democracy, and tyranny. To interpret all these sections in detail goes beyond the scope of the analysis here. Instead, I offer here a synthesis of Socrates' basic understanding of the well-ordered state, the guardians who govern it, and how these guardians are to be identified and cultivated as guardians for the good of the society as a whole. Perhaps the best place to begin in this synthesis is with Socrates' "Myth of the Metals" in Book 3.

Scholars of religion point to the "Myth of the Metals" as indicative of Plato's functional theory of religion. That is, religious myth and story serve a useful function in society whether or not they are factually or historically true. The "truths" carried in myth or story are metaphysical or philosophical truths that obtain despite the lack of factuality in the story itself. Socrates' metals story is such a myth, a fantastic, imaginative origin myth that illustrates a philosophical truth about reality, in this case about the differences in human gifts and abilities, or what Socrates refers to as people's natural abilities. The myth goes like this: All human beings have mother earth as their common source. However, the gods placed metals of gold, silver, and iron into the earth such that while all people emerge from the same source, they are differentiated from each other by containing within themselves gold, silver, or iron. Some people "contain" or "are" gold, while others are silver or iron. So, the myth explains in story form a truth that occurs in human reality. The mixture of the metals across common humanity provides for the fact that while two "gold" parents most likely will give birth to "gold" offspring, they might have "silver" or "iron" offspring. No guarantee exists that gold will produce gold, or silver produce silver. Gold might produce silver, and iron may produce gold. In Socrates' scheme, the guardians are gold, the soldiers are silver, and the craftsmen and farmers are iron. All roles are necessary and form part of the complete whole of society, but a hierarchy exists inside this basic egalitarianism: the gold are to govern all the rest, including themselves. Only those who exhibit gold characteristics are to govern; those who exhibit silver or iron must perform the social tasks fitted to those metals. Therefore, society must be structured to pay attention to the particular metals in each person so that those who display gold are not put into iron professions, and those who display iron are not put into gold professions. Chaos comes when people are placed in positions, work, or responsibility that does not fit their inherent natures or dispositions. People's natural metal, their natural talents and gifts, must be discerned and cultivated properly for the good ordering of all society.[7] This is done through education.

Throughout *The Republic*, Socrates talks about the scrutiny and testing that people must endure so that supervisors can determine their "metal," or so that, once confirmed, the "metal" in a person is developed and actualized fully. Everyone receives a basic education but then moves eventually into specialized studies once their natural abilities and dispositions come into view. At every level, people receive the education designed to bring out the best humanity in them as well as the fullest expression of their metal. The best education also achieves a balance between the soul and the body. Socrates explains in Book 3 that those who receive excessive training in music and poetry at the expense of physical or athletic training become soft, feeble, and spiritless. Conversely, those who receive only athletic education without cultivation of the soul for beauty become aggressive and seek to address every issue with violence and savagery.[8] Human beings are multi-faceted and must be educated as such to achieve their fullest potential as humans and as beings with particular gifts or "metals" unique to them.

Those with the gifts for guardianship, of course, receive the most strenuous and highly advanced education because the responsibility for the governance of the entire state rests on their shoulders. Socrates spends most of Books 2 and 3 discussing the kind of education the guardians must receive. These sections are some of the most debated passages in *The Republic* because Socrates calls for a rigid and carefully constructed educational curriculum for guardians that appears to be censored and limiting to many living in the contemporary West. Socrates claims in these sections that the guardians must not be exposed to certain kinds of literature, music, or playwriting because they tend to create certain qualities of the soul that ultimately undermine the guardians' ability to discern the good and govern properly. Many classic works of the ancient Greek world, such as the works of Homer and Hesiod, are not among what is allowed for the guardians because they portray positively heroes like Achilles or even the gods behaving in less than positive ways. Certain roles in dramatic works are off-limits to would-be guardians because to play such roles in a theater production would involve them imitating or mimicking immoral or problematic behaviors, and this could develop in their souls a capacity for such behaviors. The souls of the guardians must be safeguarded and cultivated carefully from early childhood so that in their inmost being they are attuned to goodness, beauty, order, and justice. Their role as guardians demands this quality of soul and all care must be taken to create that capacity in them from the beginning and to preserve it once cultivated. In Book 2, Socrates says of the young guardians: "At this tender age they are the most impressionable and therefore most likely to adopt any and all models set before them."[9] Later, he defends censorship of certain poetry and other artistic expression:

> In this way we could protect our guardians from growing up in the presence of evil, in a veritable pasture of poisonous herbs where by grazing at will, little by little and day by day, they

should unwittingly accumulate a huge mass of corruption in their souls.[10]

At all times, educators are mindful that it is the soul of people, especially of the guardians, which is being cultivated. Socrates claims that because education happens at the level of the soul, music and arts education is perhaps a most important component of the curriculum. He explains to his student Glaucon:

> That is why education in poetry and music is first in importance, Glaucon. Rhythm and harmonies have the greatest influence on the soul; they penetrate into its inmost regions and there hold fast. If the soul is rightly trained, they bring grace. If not, they bring the contrary. One who is properly educated in these matters would most quickly perceive and deplore the absence or perversion of beauty in art or nature. With true good taste he would instead delight in beautiful things, praising them and welcoming them into his soul. He would nourish them and would himself come to be beautiful and good. While still young and still unable to understand why, he will reject and hate what is ugly. Then, later, when reason comes to one so educated, his affinity for what is good and beautiful will lead him to recognize and welcome her.[11]

The soul is the point here, or the inner self, what some today might be more inclined to call character. This must be developed at every point, through every access, and in every component of the curriculum. Like Confucian scholars, Socrates' guardians receive intensive education in many disciplines, including music, poetry, gymnastics, mathematics, and many other areas, all with the objective of raising individuals attuned in their deepest selves to justice, goodness, and harmony. Only such individuals can be trusted with guardianship of the entire state; only with such people at its helm does the ship of state sail safely in the often rough waters of the world.

Such an understanding of education for all people, especially the guardians, comes to form a central definition for justice, according to Socrates, which is a preoccupation of the entire conversation in *The Republic*. From Book 1 onward, the discussion returns again and again to the concept of justice and how to define it. Toward the end of Book 4, after spending two entire books on guardian education, Socrates asserts a definition of justice completely intertwined with the model of education he has elucidated. He says:

> Then justice is nothing else than the power that brings forth well-governed men and well-governed cities . . . The reality is that justice is not a matter of external behavior but the way a man privately and truly governs himself. The just man does not permit the various parts of his soul to interfere with one another or usurp each other's functions. He has set his own life in order. He is his own master and his own law. He has become a friend to himself. He will have brought into tune the three parts of his soul: high, middle, and low, like the three major notes of a musical scale, and all the intervals between. When he has brought all this together in temperance and harmony, he will have made himself one man instead of many. Only then will he be ready to do whatever he does in society: making money, training the body, involving himself in politics or in business transactions. In all the public activities in which he is engaged he will call just and beautiful only that conduct which harmonizes with and preserves his own inner order which we have just described. And the knowledge that understands the meaning and importance of such conduct he will call wisdom.[12]

Justice itself, then, depends on people throughout the various professions and roles in society who have been educated since childhood on the precepts of beauty and goodness. Moreover, the society that depends on such people to govern it must itself be structured to generate those selfsame types of people for its furtherance; thus, the central role education plays in society. Education is the mechanism through which is developed the highest and best of human capacity, and the best forms of education are those that, no matter what their immediate subject matter, have as their chief objective the cultivation of the human soul attuned to justice, beauty, and goodness. Without such individuals at all its levels, society is lost.

Gülen, from within an Islamic perspective many centuries removed from both Confucius and Socrates, presents a largely resonant theory of education, the soul, and human development. He, like his ancient colleagues, understands the human self as a being comprised of corporeal, mental, and spiritual components. Each of these components must be developed properly to achieve full human potential, and this development occurs through education. Gülen explains:

> We are creatures comprised of not only a body or mind or feelings or spirit; rather, we are harmonious compositions of all of these elements. Each of us is a body writhing in a net of needs, as well as a mind that has more subtle and vital needs than the body, and is driven by anxieties about the past and future . . . Moreover, each person is a creature of feelings that cannot be satisfied by the mind, and a creature of spirit, through which we acquire our essential human identity. Each individual is all of these. When a man or a woman, around whom all systems and efforts revolve, is considered and evaluated as a creature with all these aspects, and when all our needs are fulfilled, we will reach true happiness. At this point, true human progress and evolvement in relation to our essential being is only possible with education.[13]

Here, we see resonance with Socrates' definition of the human self with three distinct parts, the mind or soul, the drives, and the body. All the parts must be developed properly, and must function in their proper order within a person in order for full human actualization. Gülen expresses a similar sentiment in this passage, namely, that each man or woman is a complex of components that must be developed in themselves and must be organized harmoniously within the self for human progress to occur.

This passage and others like it form part of a larger discussion of history in which Gülen traces the development of civilizations both East and West. He argues that although Western civilization has dominated the world for the last several centuries, and has provided the leading edge in science and technology, the worldview of the modern West is materialistic and, thus, lacking. That is, the Western perspective views human beings in largely materialistic terms, and seeks to fulfill human achievement in those reduced terms.

Sacrificed in such an approach are the other dimensions of human being, which are spiritual, and this sacrifice has created many social crises. Part of Gülen's vision for the future involves combining the best of Western culture, which is scientific and technological, with the best of Eastern culture, which is spiritual and moral, in order to create a more fully evolved and holistic human culture that will take all reality into a new era.[14]

For Gülen, as for Socrates and Confucius, no individual or society reaches its fullest potential without education. Gülen sees education as the means by which people become the true beings God created them to be; thus, to become educated is life's most important task. He says:

> The main duty and purpose of human life is to seek under-standing. The effort of doing so, known as education, is a per-fecting process through which we earn, in the spiritual, intellec-tual, and physical dimensions of our beings, the rank appointed for us as the perfect pattern of creation . . . Our principal duty in life is to acquire perfection and purity in our thinking, per-ceptions, and belief. By fulfilling our duty of servanthood to the Creator, Nourisher, and Protector, and by penetrating the mystery of creation through our potential and abilities, we seek to attain the rank of true humanity and become worthy of a blissful, eternal life in another, exalted world.[15]

Here, Gülen places learning and education at the most funda-mental level of human purpose. In a phrase, the purpose of human life is to become fully human, and that happens through learning and knowledge. Gülen, as a Muslim, places this within the larger context of service to God, but one could place it just as easily into a more Aristotelian context in which the purpose or function of everything is to be itself fully and perfectly, and everything is natu-rally endowed with the internal components and capacities to be perfectly itself given the proper context. Human beings are born with the capacity to become fully human and, for Gülen (as for Aristotle, Socrates, Confucius, and many others), the inborn mechanism for becoming fully human is our capacity to learn through education. Gülen says:

> Since "real" life is only possible through knowledge, those who have neglected learning and teaching are considered to be "dead," even when they are biologically alive. We were created to learn and to communicate what we have learned to others.[16]

Gülen speaks throughout his work about the need for general education for all people in order for a civilization to function. He claims that people are only "civilized" to the extent that they are educated, especially in the traditional values of a particular culture. Cohesion in life at all levels comes via education of all citizens of a nation or state in a common worldview and core of values. The transnational Gülen movement, however, focuses on education far beyond a given set of cultural values or norms. The nearly one thousand schools (at the time of this writing) run by Gülen movement participants which are operating all over the world educate children and young adults in the full range of academic disciplines: science, mathematics, history, language, literature, social or cultural studies, art, music, and more. People inspired by Gülen's teachings opened schools in Turkey after the government allowed the operating of private schools as long as they adhered to a state-mandated curriculum and submitted themselves to state review. Schools set up by Gülen movement participants in other countries operate with the same basic educational approach as the schools in Turkey, but with increasing influence of the indigenous countries' national culture and values. Gülen himself has very little, if any, contact with the schools and, in fact, is not even aware of the exact number of schools, or even their names. His own early example as an educator, as well as his ideas about education, global community, human progress, and so on, have simply inspired a generation of people to raise up schools all over Turkey, Central Asia, Europe, Africa, and elsewhere to combat the perennial problems of ignorance, poverty, and schism.

The basic structure and character of the schools is such that they are financed by voluntary organizations, community groups, and student fees; local administrators assist with infrastructure; and the teachers work within a mindset of service to others, often for low salaries. As I mentioned in the introduction to this book, I have visited many of these schools throughout Turkey, and have met with the sponsors of the schools, that is, the local businessmen and local community leaders who joined together to create the schools in their respective regions. In many instances, the schools are the most modern architectural structure in the area; the walls of the school are lined with photographs of students receiving medals at various national and international academic competitions and being visited by an array of Turkish government ministers and members of Parliament; the classroom, laboratory, and office facilities are highly functional and professional looking even when being used by hundreds of excited students; the students are bright, outgoing, and eager to practice their English with American visitors; the principals, administrators, and teachers are focused, dedicated, and proud of their schools and students, and many of them live on the premises with the students in the schools that offer boarding. I shared meals with many Turkish families who send their children to these schools, and I asked them the same question in each city, each region: Why do you send your children to this school? The answer was the same every time. They send them because of the dedication of the teachers, the quality of the curriculum, and the overall vision that the school, through its teachers, promotes with regard to global humanity, education, tolerance, and dialogue.

Gülen's educational vision involves not only schools, but also families, communities, and media. All major components of society must be aligned in the work of educating the youth in all beneficial knowledge.[*] The stakes are very high because the future of any nation or civilization depends on its youth. Gülen says:

---

[*] This resonates with Mill's idea expressed in an earlier chapter that all social institutions must be designed to cultivate or "educate" people's innate capacities for higher pleasures.

> People who want to guarantee their future cannot be indifferent to how their children are educated. The family, school, environment, and mass media should all co-operate to ensure the desired result . . . In particular, the mass media should contribute to the education of the young generation by following the education policy approved by the community. The school must be as perfect as possible with respect to its curriculum, the scientific and moral standards of the teachers, and its physical conditions. A family must provide the necessary warmth and atmosphere in which to raise children.[17]

Here, we see Gülen expressing concerns highly resonant with those Socrates expresses in *The Republic*. As we saw above, Socrates goes so far as to argue for censorship of the poets and musicians, ancient Greece's mass media, so that the guardians are exposed only to artistic expression that will nurture their souls. While Gülen nowhere advocates censorship in the way Socrates does, he shares with Socrates a general concern for proper education in order to achieve the fullest actualization of humanity, which includes the support of parents and the community, the environment of the school, the topics taught, and the moral standards of the teachers.

We can further see the importance of education for all of society when Gülen speaks of the role of consultation in Islam in particular, and in society at large. He devotes an entire chapter to the subject in *The Statue of Our Souls*, and in this chapter Gülen clearly delineates the vital role that highly educated people play in the furtherance of society, and the kinds of education needed for today's globalized world. He begins by quoting a passage from the Qur'an that places conducting affairs by mutual consultation in the same category as performing regular prayers. He goes on to cite the central importance that consultation has within Islam, so much so that a community without it is not really Muslim in the full sense. He continues by explaining how it works in Muslim society:

> Consultation is one of the prime dynamics which keep the Islamic order standing as a system. To consultation belongs the most important mission and duty of resolving affairs concerning the individual and the community, the people and the state,

science and knowledge, and economics and sociology, unless of
course there is a *nass* (divine decree; a verse of the Qur'an or a
command from the Prophet, decisive on any point in canon
law) with a clear meaning on these matters.[18]

Even rulers must conduct affairs using consultation. Consultation
is the method by which the ruler or rulers make the decisions that
impact virtually every area of life, from the individual to the communal. Gülen spends several pages outlining the scriptural passages
that support consultation, and explaining the history of its use in
Islam, and he reviews established guidelines for the practice. He
then comes to the central question of who is fit for consultation.
With whom should rulers consult? Who is qualified to serve as a
consultant? Gülen answers:

> [S]ince the matters presented for deliberation require a great
> degree of knowledge, experience, and expertise, a consultation
> committee must be comprised of people who are distinguished
> for such qualities. This can only be a committee of people of
> high caliber, who are able to resolve many matters. Especially
> today, as life has become more intricate and complicated, as the
> world has globalized, and every problem has become an all-
> encompassing, planetary problem, it is vital that those compe-
> tent in natural sciences, engineering, and technology, which are
> most of the time considered to be good and proper by Muslims,
> should participate alongside those men of high caliber who
> know Islamic essence, reality, spirit, and sciences. Consultation
> can be carried out with qualified people from the different world-
> ly sciences, knowledge, and other required fields, insofar as
> decisions taken are supervised by the religious authorities for
> the compatibility or accord of what they suggest with Islam.[19]

In this passage, we begin to see the high standard people have
to meet in order to function as consultants. Important to remember is that Gülen articulates a vision for an Islamic society, which
he believes is the best kind of society. Whether one agrees with him
or not is irrelevant. Our point here is that within his envisioned
society, education is absolutely vital for all people to attain the basics
of human existence. Moreover, high levels of education are needed

by an elite cadre of individuals who are to serve as consultants to rulers on particular issues, or who may serve as rulers themselves in some capacity. Gülen explains further:

> According to different circumstances and eras, the conduct and composition of the consultative committee might change, but the qualifications and the attributes of those select people, such as people from knowledge, justice, social education and experience, wisdom, and sagacity, must never change.[20]

More often than not, these consultants will be the "ideal humans" or "people of heart" Gülen describes elsewhere in his work and that we discussed in the previous chapter. The consultants are those the schools inspired by Gülen are designed to educate, young people who will go into the world with a virtuous character as well as a high level of academic training in their various professions. Some of those young people will achieve extraordinary levels of success and wisdom, and will be called upon to serve as consultants. In doing so, they will be the generation of "ideal people" who are to usher in a new social reality that will mend the false bifurcation between science and religion, that will mesh East and West, and that will offer a whole new way of life to the world.

For Gülen, there is no other way to structure society that deserves to be called "human" and certainly no other way that can be called "Islamic." Human beings have within them the capacities to achieve perfection as humans, and those who internalize and actualize that perfection in themselves must influence society, as rulers or consultants, or grassroots community leaders. For any of these things to happen, people must be educated in an intentional, proper way. The schools of the transnational Gülen movement are contemporary initiatives in this endeavor, and they seek to educate their youth from all sectors of society to become highly trained and virtuous people who, like Confucian superior men, influence everything and everyone around them with the force (*te*) of their knowledge, goodness, and beauty.

Each of our trialogue participants presents a powerful vision of what is possible on the human social and political level. The power of this vision is due, in no small part, to the spiritual or non-material quality that they all, in their own way and within their own cultural and linguistic rubrics, acknowledge as a central part of humanness. This "soul" quality is what, in their respective views, distinguishes humans from the rest of the animal creation. All three firmly believe in our inherent powers to develop our inborn capacities for human perfection, although all three acknowledge that many people will never use these powers. Their belief in this power, used or not, is what makes Confucius, Socrates, and Gülen humanists in the broad sense of the term. They believe in human power to become fully and ideally human.

Further, because people can do it, they must do it. These men are not fatalists or determinists. They do not see people, individually or collectively, as pawns of history or of fate. Gülen, in particular, even taking into account his view of an all-powerful, all-knowing God, exhorts his readers to take responsibility for themselves and for the world. The challenge of responsibility is a great challenge for any age, but perhaps our current age of rapid change and mass violence calls out for us to meet it more than any other. We turn now in the next chapter to this theme of responsibility.

5

Gülen and Sartre on Responsibility

The last two chapters focused on the ideal human as conceived by Confucius, Socrates, and Gülen, and the role that such ideal humans play in state or national governance, and in community leadership. We concluded by affirming that all three thinkers were humanists in the broad sense of the term, primarily because they deeply support the idea that human beings are capable of actualizing in themselves a moral and intellectual ideal, that a human society can progress as a whole toward that ideal on a collective level, and that education is the principal mechanism through which this is accomplished. The entire discussion of the previous two chapters relies on a fundamental conviction about human beings which Gülen discusses throughout his work, and to which he is principally committed in his writings: the idea that human beings are responsible for the world.

Human responsibility for the world, for one's own life and the lives of others, for society, and for the future is a constant theme across the centuries of humanism and in much religious discourse. Indeed, the central principles of humanism about the power, capacity, ability, and beauty of human beings individually and collectively make no sense, or at least are vulnerable to the charge of moral vacuity, unless accompanied by a strong belief in human responsibility in and for the world. To affirm human power and ability in the world but not human responsibility to employ that power in the creation of the parts of the world amenable to human intervention seems illogical at best, or cynical at worst. Humanistic philosophy—that is, a belief in the ability and responsibility of human beings to be creators of the world in some meaningful sense—has been, therefore, the back on which people and societies have accomplished some of the greatest of human achievements. So many wonders of the world in art, literature, architecture, social and political philosophy and application, medical science, and other areas exist because people believed in their power to create new things, develop new perspectives, and achieve new breakthroughs. Some saw their power as given to them by God or gods and viewed their service and achievements as worship of God; others viewed their power from a non-religious perspective. In both cases, people claimed their power, from wherever it derived, as well as their responsibility to use that power for the good of society.

For the final dialogue in this book on the theme of responsibility, I could choose as Gülen's dialogue partner any number of humanists from the long lines of both the Western and Eastern traditions. Many philosophers, writers, statesmen, theorists, and thinkers from many centuries and across cultures have dwelt on the theme of responsibility to varying degrees in their work. Even those with strong theological commitments to an all-powerful, all-knowing, predestining God could make this list of those who assert a strong notion of human responsibility for the world. (Gülen himself falls into this category.) For this last dialogue, however, I have chosen the chief expositor for one of the most influential schools of philosophy in the twentieth century, and one who defends more than anyone else the notion of human responsibility for virtually everything. That philosopher is Jean Paul Sartre from the existentialist school of thought.

Immediately, questions arise concerning this choice, legitimate questions that we must address before we proceed. First of all, it might seem problematic to pair Gülen with an atheist such as Sartre. How could any resonance or dialogue exist between an atheist, on the one hand, and a Muslim scholar, on the other? Why should we want there to be any dialogue between them? Atheists and theists, especially monotheists, commonly denounce each other and, thus, are not interested in dialogue. This, however, is the very reason why such a dialogue must occur, even if in this case it occurs only in the pages of a book. The inherently free nature of human conscience virtually guarantees that atheists and monotheists, and all shades of belief or unbelief in between, will continue to exist in the world as they do now and probably always have. Mutual denunciations of atheists and believers do nothing but undermine peaceful co-existence in today's globalized and staggeringly diverse world. We cannot afford to allow mutual denunciations to become or remain the norm among people who disagree on matters of belief. We must encourage dialogue even among those who have, or seem to have, nothing to say to each other.

Second, Gülen himself openly criticizes Sartre and existentialism. In *The Statue of Our Souls*, Gülen places existentialism on a long list of aberrant "-isms" that swept through Turkey and the West in the late nineteenth and twentieth centuries, including Marxism, Durkheimism, Leninism, and Maoism. He says of the Turkish youth of that period:

> Some consoled themselves with the dreams of Communism and the dictatorship of the proletariat, some went and sank into Freudian complexes, some lost their minds to existentialism and became entangled with Sartre, some slobbered over the sacred by quoting Marcuse, some started to waste their lives among the delirium of Camus . . . [1]

Clearly, Gülen is not a fan of existentialism, or of two of its chief proponents, Sartre and Camus. Therefore, how and why should we place Sartre into any kind of meaningful conversation with Gülen's ideas when Gülen has such a low opinion of Sartre's ideas? This is simply another version of the first question. Gülen rejects existentialism on many points; Sartre, were he alive, would reject many of Gülen's ideas. Again, however, this does not preclude a dialogue between them. If it does, then the entire project of dialogue, so central to the Gülen movement, is severely undermined because only those who largely agree could dialogue with each other. Genuine relationship and respect can exist between people who strongly disagree with each other's viewpoints, as do Gülen and Sartre, or any other believer and atheist. Moreover, Gülen can fulfill his duty as a Muslim scholar obligated by the Qur'an to deplore atheism by rejecting atheistic ideas but still respecting the person for simply being a human being who possesses inherent worth and dignity. Dialogue is the means by which we maintain our focus on the humanity of others, even when, or perhaps especially when, we strongly disagree with their ideas. Finding commonalities amidst radical difference is a proven strategy for peaceful coexistence among people who largely disagree. Such difficult dialogues may, in fact, be the most important ones to have. So, with this in mind, let us turn to Sartre and Gülen to see what connections, if any, can possibly exist between their ideas.

Sartre's ideas, and those of existentialism as a whole, suffer from the popularity the existentialist movement had in the middle part of the twentieth century. That is, it became so popular as a philosophy, both in France and throughout the West, that it became even a fashion fad. Existentialism was, and still is, spread in the vernacular by those whose interpretations reflect a popular, "mass" understanding of its ideas, rather than a sustained and thorough reading of its central themes as they are expressed across the work of the school's many representatives. This is complicated, as well, by the fact that most existentialists do not agree with each other on all points, or on many points at all in some cases. Most people view Sartre, one of the more prolific writers in the school, as the central expositor of the entire existentialist perspective, a position that he accepts to some extent in certain moments of his work.

Sartre was well aware of the limited and often outright erroneous interpretations of existentialism, and the claims made in the popular culture about the school of thought as a whole. He addresses these concerns in an essay commonly called "Existentialism as a Humanism" or simply "Existentialism" in a larger work published in 1957 called *Existentialism and Human Emotions*. In this excerpt,

Sartre identifies the chief mistakes people make in interpreting existentialism, or in identifying its central assertions about human reality. As he defends existentialism against these problematic claims, we see a vision of human beingness in the world quite distinct from the most common renderings of existentialism. Sartre articulates a theme of human responsibility that inspires passionate action and powerful affirmation of human ability to shape the world. Sartre stops just short of using the term "duty" to describe the relationship of humans toward the world that they can shape. However, the spirit of the word is there, even if the letter is not. Those who choose to live in the world and not take responsibility for it are living a less than fully human life, and they are cowards. This assertion, along with others like it, form a core of ideas that, as it turns out, resonate quite powerfully with selected themes in Gülen's thought.

Sartre summarizes the charges against existentialism at the beginning of the essay, then goes on to define and explain his version of it. As he explains existentialism's basic components, he answers the most common charges leveled against it. The charges are simple and well-known, based on the popular understanding of existentialism: that it encourages passivity or quietism; that it dwells on and revels in everything ugly about life; and that it denies the seriousness of human undertakings. In short, people criticize and reject French atheistic existentialism because they interpret it as a kind of nihilism, or celebration of nothingness. Nothing ultimate exists—no God, no absolute values, no fixed or essential meaning for life or people; therefore, there is no point in becoming socially or politically active, nor in undertaking sustained efforts to improve the world or to achieve breakthroughs in knowledge.

Sartre rejects, even lightly mocks, this understanding of existentialism, and spends the first part of his answer to these charges by defining existentialism accurately. He says that all the varieties of existentialism, the Christian and the atheistic, assert one common claim: that existence precedes essence. Sartre, as a defender of the atheistic variety, says that this claim especially holds true for his version of existentialism. "Essence" here refers to a purpose, meaning, or nature. Most inanimate objects are created to fulfill a purpose or meaning that exists in the minds of their creators. A paper-cutter, for example, comes into existence after its inventor designs and manufactures it in response to a purpose, goal, or meaning the inventor has for the paper-cutter. The inventor needs something to cut paper, but nothing exists to do this, so he invents a paper-cutter whose purpose and meaning in existence is to cut paper. Its essence precedes its existence. Most people, says Sartre, think of God in this way with reference to human beings: God created human beings to fulfill His purpose and their meaning is tied to that purpose. Their essence precedes their existence, just like the paper-cutter. Meaning, purpose, and nature are predetermined by their creators in both instances. Entities come into existence and, in the case of humans, seek to learn that purpose in order to find happiness.

Sartre, however, is an atheist, which means that there is no God in whose mind human meaning, purpose, and nature—human "essence"—live before He creates the humans themselves. Since there is no God, humans simply come into being, thrown into existence first, and their essence comes later. For humans, existence precedes essence, and this is the first principle of existentialism. Sartre explains:

> What is meant here by saying that existence precedes essence? It means that, first of all, man exists, turns up, appears on the scene, and, only afterwards, defines himself. If man, as the existentialist conceives him, is indefinable, it is because at first he is nothing. Only afterwards will he be something, and he himself will have made what he will be. Thus, there is no human nature, since there is no God to conceive it. Not only is man what he conceives himself to be, but he is also only what he wills himself to be after this thrust toward existence. Man is nothing else but what he makes of himself. Such is the first principle of existentialism.[2]

So, there exists no predetermined meaning or purpose for human life or lives because there is no God to have conceived it. Human beings simply exist, are thrown into being, and must make for themselves their purpose, meaning, and nature. Already in this first principle, we see the seeds of responsibility that Sartre sows into his philosophy of human beings, especially since human beings come into existence as thinking beings and, as they cognitively develop, become self-aware. Sartre continues:

> Man is at the start a plan which is aware of itself, rather than a patch of moss, a piece of garbage, or a cauliflower; nothing exists prior to this plan; there is nothing in heaven; man will be what he will have planned to be . . . But if existence really does precede essence, man is responsible for what he is. Thus, existentialism's first move is to make every man aware of what he is and to make the full responsibility of his existence rest on him. And when we say that a man is responsible for himself, we do not only mean that he is responsible for his own individuality, but that he is responsible for all men.[3]

Two important issues for our discussion emerge from this passage. First, the responsibility of which Sartre speaks extends past any individual human being to all human beings. This claim is tied to Sartre's understanding of subjectivity; that is, at all times human beings are tied to the world, to the human world, to the world of human being. We can never get outside the world, outside our own humanness, outside to an "objective" perspective in isolation from the world and others. We all exist, by nature, in the world with others, as a part of the world, in communal human beingness. Therefore, when we choose for our lives and take responsibility for creating our lives, we are not creating just for ourselves alone; we are creating for everyone because we are tied to everyone. We are rooted in subjectivity. To choose is to advance the choice not just for ourselves individually but for everyone. Sartre says, "In creating the man that we want to be, there is not a single one of our acts which does not at the same time create an image of man as we think we ought to be."[4]

A second important point from the lengthy quote above concerns Sartre's definition of a human being. In the quote, he distinguishes human beings from "a patch of moss, a piece of garbage,

or a cauliflower." Human beings are not merely objects among other objects, left to the hands of fate, the whims of blind bodily instinct,
destiny, or weather. Later in the essay, he makes this point more
strongly. He says of the theory of existentialism:

> [T]his theory is the only one which gives man dignity, the only
> one which does not reduce him to an object. The effect of all
> materialism is to treat all men, including the one philosophiz-
> ing, as objects, that is, as an ensemble of determined reactions
> in no way distinguished from the ensemble of qualities and
> phenomena which constitute a table or a chair or a stone. We
> definitely wish to establish the human realm as an ensemble of
> values distinct from the material realm.[5]

Here, Sartre is separating existentialism from materialism,
which Gülen and many others with a religious perspective reject so
definitively either as a symptom of spiritual sickness, an aspect of
atheism, or a reductionist account of human life. Sartre rejects it,
too, albeit through different channels of argumentation. Sartre's
existentialism does not allow people to be at the level of stones,
chairs, or pieces of moss. Instead, it insists that humans are much
more than this, not because they are made by God with a purpose
or meaning, but because from birth onward we clearly exhibit in
our own lives the capacity for consciousness, self-consciousness,
and self-self-consciousness, which is unlike any other living being.
Unlike other beings, we think, in the full Cartesian sense of the
word, which includes self-thinking, or thinking upon the self. This
marks a categorical difference between humans and all other living
things. Moreover, it is this domain in human beingness that gives
rise to the creation of values, ideals, and meaning. Being people in
this condition, and rooted in human subjectivity, we must say to
ourselves at the outset of every action if we are being honest and
responsible in the world, "Am I really the kind of man who has the
right to act in such a way that humanity might guide itself by my
actions?"[6] Sartre says not to ask that question is to live in what he
calls "bad faith" with oneself and with the world.

Clearly, a depressed, weary, passive, and isolated person is not what Sartre has in mind here as someone who is taking responsibility for themselves and for the world. Such a person shirks their responsibility for their own life, as well as others' lives, with a kind of weary throwing up of the hands: "What can be done? Nothing." Quite the contrary, according to Sartre, much can be done! Moreover, we are the only ones to do it, and we are "doing it" even as we sit and say we are not and deny our responsibility for it by saying we are just born this way, or we could not help it, or fate has decreed it. Resigned passivity is the result of a philosophy that relinquishes human life to fate and materialistic determinism. Existentialism, on the other hand, rejects fatalism and materialistic determinism and sees all of human life as an arena for action and responsibility, rooted in the claim that there is no one but us, we will be what we make ourselves to be, and the world will be what we make of it, nothing more and nothing less. Sartre spends much of his essay describing the "marks" of living fully inside this awareness of responsibility and action, and he labels these with three words: anguish, forlornness, and despair. Misinterpreted, these concepts leave us depressed and passive. Properly understood, they have us out in the world trying to actualize our best plans for ourselves and for the world.

By anguish, Sartre refers simply to the experience one has when living in complete acknowledgment of responsibility. He says:

> What that [anguish] means is this: the man who involves himself and who realizes that he is not only the person he chooses to be, but also a lawmaker who is, at the same time, choosing all mankind as well as himself, cannot help escape the feeling of his total and deep responsibility. Of course, there are many people who are not anxious; but we claim that they are hiding their anxiety, that they are fleeing from it.[7]

Both of these, fleeing from the anguish itself, or from the entire notion of being responsible, constitute bad faith in Sartre's view. He claims that anyone in a leadership position knows this anguish, such as a military commander who chooses whether to lead his soldiers into a battle, knowing that upon his choice depend the lives of his men. Of course, he could avoid responsibility and pass it on to his superiors, saying that in leading the men to battle he was simply following orders. Sartre says, however, that the commander interpreted the orders and decided whether or not to act on them. Therefore, he is responsible for his choice. Not to feel anguish in this position is not to take responsibility. Moreover, feeling the anguish does not allow for inaction on the part of the commander; he must still choose whether or not to send his soldiers into battle. Far from being an excuse for inaction, his anguish is the very condition of his action. This anguish, Sartre says, is "not a curtain separating us from the action, but is a part of the action itself."[8]

Forlornness is very simple as well, says Sartre. By forlornness, he says "we mean only that God does not exist and that we have to face all the consequences of this."[9] Sartre rejects the modernist tendency in the West to claim atheism, yet still act as if a transcendent realm of morality, purpose, and meaning exists. In such a scheme, God is an outdated concept to be abandoned, yet the values and meanings grounded in God's existence can somehow still have the same ultimacy as if God existed, so society can proceed comfortably forward. Sartre finds this not only illogical, but also irresponsible. He says:

> The existentialist, on the contrary, thinks it very distressing that God does not exist because all possibility of finding values in a heaven of ideas disappears along with Him; there can no longer be an *a priori* Good, since there is no infinite and perfect consciousness to think it . . . Dostoievsky said "If God didn't exist, everything would be possible." That is the very starting point of existentialism. Indeed, everything is permissible if God does not exist, and as a result man is forlorn because neither within him nor without does he find anything to cling to. He can't start making excuses for himself.[10]

The last sentence here is the point, and it is easy to miss. Sartre is not saying that we should just do anything we please because since God does not exist, nothing has any divinely appointed value, and no notion of the Good exists. Instead, he is saying that when we live in full awareness of these facts, we clearly see that we, not God, are responsible for everything. We have no recourse to relinquishing events in our lives or the world to "God's will" or "God's plan" or something of this nature. We decide what is good and valuable, not God. We feel the anguish that comes with this position, the incredible responsibility for everything, the forlornness or aloneness that is ours in the world. Not to feel this, or to try not to feel this, is "making excuses" for ourselves.

Sartre goes so far as to say that even if God does exist, our human situation is not changed. He gives several examples in the essay of believers who live as if God has chosen their path for them, or as if the values they live and choose are grounded firmly in God: a woman who hears spiritual voices commanding her to do things; a student who gets life guidance from God via a priest; a Catholic who acts based on signs from God; and a Jesuit who sees the hand of God in the circumstances of his life. In all these instances, Sartre says, people are evading responsibility, not because they dare to believe in God, but because they refuse to see their own responsibility in their belief. They do not see that they themselves determine what is or is not a sign from God, whether the voices heard are from God or the devil, whether the priest is right or not, how the sacred text is to be interpreted, and so on. Even if God exists and sends angels to speak to us, to give us revelation that we write down word for word, we are the ones who decide if the angels are worth listening to, and how to interpret the words they give us. In the end, we are still responsible. We cannot make excuses for ourselves, and we cannot let ourselves off the hook. Sartre, at the end of his essay, explains that existentialism spends no time defending its atheism, mainly because in the end it makes no difference with regard to human responsibility. He says:

> Existentialism isn't so atheistic that it wears itself out showing that God doesn't exist. Rather, it declares that even if God did exist, that would change nothing. There you've got our point of view. Not that we believe God exists, but we think that the problem of His existence is not the issue.[11]

Either way, we are responsible for the world, our values, our meaning, and our purpose. There is no escaping this, and to try to do so is to live in bad faith with the world.

Finally, by despair, Sartre means that we must act in the world, as wholly responsible agents, without ever knowing if our actions will accomplish the desired results. We cannot, as Hegel does, rely on a transcendent *Geist* to guide history toward the ever higher goals of our actions. Nor can we rely on innate human goodness, or the ubiquity of Truth, or some such notion, to ensure that our actions will bring about our desired future. Nothing is guaranteed, says Sartre:

> Given that men are free and that tomorrow they will freely decide what man will be, I cannot be sure that, after my death, fellow-fighters will carry on my work to bring it to its maximum perfection. Tomorrow, after my death, some men may decide to set us Fascism, and the others may be cowardly and muddled enough to let them do it. Fascism will be the human reality, so much the worse for us. Actually, things will be as man will have decided they are to be.[12]

We have no guarantees that our actions will bear fruit after we are dead and out of the arena of action. Some would say, then, that this fact alone justifies inaction and passivity, and ask why one should bother to act if it is possible that our actions will not bear fruit. Again, Sartre says we are responsible. We remain responsible for the entire world even though we are limited by our own mortality. Thus, we experience despair. Sartre says:

> Does this mean that I should abandon myself to quietism? No. First, I should involve myself; then, act on the old saw, "Nothing ventured, nothing gained." Nor does it mean that I shouldn't belong to a party, but rather that I shall have no illusions and shall do what I can. For example, suppose I ask myself, "Will socialization, as such, ever come about?" I know nothing about it. All I know is that I'm going to do everything in my power to bring it about. Beyond that, I can't count on anything. Quietism is the attitude of people who say, "Let others do what I can't do." The doctrine I am presenting here is the very opposite

of quietism, since it declares, "There is no reality except in action." Moreover, it goes further, since it adds, "Man is nothing else than his plan; he exists only to the extent that he fulfills himself; he is therefore nothing else than the ensemble of his acts, nothing else than his life."[13]

So, like anguish, despair is the condition of our actions and cannot be an excuse for inaction if we remain responsible for the world. The image in this passage is of people who give themselves fully to the tasks at hand, to those projects and plans to which they are most committed and find their highest fulfillment, all the while knowing that there are no guarantees that the work will be completed, but knowing also that they are wholly responsible for the world, no matter the anguish, forlornness, and despair.

Important to mention here is that being responsible, and having anguish, forlornness, and despair is not inherently a life of misery. Sartre goes so far as to say that existentialism is a kind of optimism, albeit a tough one. Life lived inside responsibility certainly involves sacrifice and suffering, but this does not equate to lifelong misery or depression. Life lived inside responsibility is a life of action, of achievement, of fulfillment of projects, a life of powerful creation. It is truly an invented life and an invented world, and it is invented by us, by human beings, beings distinct from all others because of our self-consciousness and our inner domain of valuation and conscience. Most people, of course, are horrified by the possibility of living such a created or invented life. They do not want to take full responsibility for their lives or the world, and prefer instead to make fate, God, circumstances, nature, or biology responsible for their lives. Being confronted with the horror of their responsibility, they flee into bad faith and lash out at the school of thought that asserts their responsibility.

Sartre lived his own life as a social and political activist, a philosopher, a teacher, a soldier, and an involved citizen consistent with this idea of responsibility. Sartre says near the end of his essay:

Thus, I think we have answered a number of the charges concerning existentialism. You see that it cannot be taken for a

> philosophy of quietism, since it defines man in terms of action; nor for a pessimistic description of man—there is no doctrine more optimistic, since man's destiny is within himself; nor for an attempt to discourage man from acting, since it tells him that the only hope is in his acting and that action is the only thing that enables a man to live. Consequently, we are dealing here with an ethics of action and involvement.[14]

Gülen does not reject Sartre for his views about responsibility. In fact, Gülen and Sartre find powerful resonance on this theme, even while disagreeing on virtually everything else. As a Muslim and expositing his ideas completely within an Islamic context, Gülen speaks about issues of human agency and responsibility in the world in a way parallel to that of almost all theologians in the great monotheisms when addressing these topics. Indeed, these topics provide fodder for rich discussion, analysis, and debate over the centuries in all of the great religions that posit an all-powerful, all-knowing God. The crux of the issue is reconciling the tension between God's will and providence, on the one hand, and human will and action, on the other. Most monotheistic theologians, especially those who posit eternal reward and punishment, do not negate human free will because doing so negates human responsibility for their actions, which calls into question the justice of eternal heaven or hell as the "reward" for human action, a belief central to both Christianity and Islam. If humans have no free will, how can they be punished or rewarded for their actions? On the other hand, positing full, free human agency seems to undermine the idea of divine providence. God is not the ultimate director of the world if humans in their free will choose another path for it. So, this tension between God's providence and human free will receives a great deal of attention in theological circles, and the attempts to reconcile the tension, or to moderate it, are numerous and various across the traditions.*

---

*   Gülen's ideas find their home in the Hanafi/Maturidi tradition which, like some schools of thought in Judaism and Christianity, seeks to harmonize divine providence and human free will by positing a divine plan premised on God's foreknowledge of human choices.

We need not discuss these here except to say that this tension or issue is in the background as Gülen exposits his notions of human responsibility in the world. Thus, he will never say, in the way of Sartre, that human beings are wholly responsible for the world as it exists in history because to do so undermines the idea of divine providence and decree, in which he very much believes. Gülen preaches the God of Islam, the all-powerful, all-knowing God who is the maker of heaven and earth, and who knows all things. All reality and existence is what it is because of divine decree, and has no being or reality at all outside of that decree. This faith commitment qualifies every statement Gülen makes about human responsibility, and it is a fundamental difference in the worldviews of Sartre and Gülen that resists mediation.

Gülen speaks about this issue, however, in a way that opens up a few channels of passage that help us understand how he can speak of the "consciousness of responsibility" in the way that he does in *The Statue of Our Souls* and elsewhere. He speaks of this issue using a key word which is translated in English as "vicegerent" or "vicegerency." Using such a word already indicates, at least in English, that he is performing a subtle balancing act with regard to divine providence and human free will. Vicegerency means management, rulership, and responsibility, to be sure. The prefix "vice," however, connotes deputization from a superior authority, even perhaps by decree. Here we have Gülen's perspective in a nutshell, along with that of many other theologians in the monotheistic traditions who are faced with the difficult challenge of reconciling divine providence and human free will. The all-knowing, all-powerful God, by decree, created existence in such a way that the human world inside this existence is affected by human agency. People either fulfill this charge or not, and suffer the consequences in this life and the next. Regardless, the infinite and, thus, mysterious (since our finite minds cannot comprehend infinity but can nevertheless be "called" by it) plans of God for the world and all existence remain fulfilled. Again, this is a delicate balancing act that may not completely resolve the tension between divine providence and human free will, but it does, perhaps, the best job of it that can be done that preserves a serious place for human agency and responsibility in the world, which is our concern here.

Gülen bases his claims for human vicegerency on the Qur'an (2:30): "I will create a vicegerent on earth."[15] As vicegerents, human beings are divine representatives in the world. Gülen says:

> If humanity is the vicegerent of God on Earth, the favorite of all His creation, the essence and substance of existence in its entirety and the brightest mirror of the Creator—and there is no doubt that this is so—then the Divine Being that has sent humanity to this realm will have given us the right, permission, and ability to discover the mysteries imbedded in the soul of the universe, to uncover the hidden power, might, and potential, to use everything to its purpose, and to be the representatives of characteristics that belong to Him, such as knowledge, will, and might.[16]

Here, we see Gülen performing the delicate balancing act mentioned above. He powerfully affirms human beings as both the creation and the mirror of God. People are both creatures and reflections, submitted to the Creator and representatives of that same Creator. This is the position of the vicegerent: submitted always to the decrees of God, and always, by that same decree, charged with representing and doing the work of that God in the world with the inner capacities that mirror those of God. Gülen further explains human vicegerency:

> Humanity's vicegerency for the Creator takes place in an unusually broad sphere that encompasses acts ranging from believing in Him and worshiping Him to understanding the mysteries within things and the cause of natural phenomena, and therefore being able to interfere in nature . . . [T]hese genuine human beings try to exercise their free will in a constructive manner, working with and developing the world, protecting the harmony between existence and humanity, reaping the bounties of the Earth and the Heavens for the benefit of humanity, trying to raise the hue, form, and flavor of life to a more humane level within the framework of the Creator's

orders and rules. This is the true nature of a vicegerent and at
the same time this is where the meaning of what it is to be a
servant and lover of God can be found.[17]

Notice the range of human action in the role of vicegerent, which
includes religious acknowledgement and worship, scientific knowledge of the natural world, modes of "interfering" with or manipu-
lating the natural world for positive ends, and improving human
life in ever richer and more humane ways. As vicegerents, human
beings are responsible for all this. They are accountable to God, as
field agents, for the fulfillment of their duties in these domains.

Gülen discusses human vicegerency at length in *The Statue of
Our Souls* in a way that seems much more spirited and radical than
in other writings. Early in the book, he takes up the discussion of
divine providence and human free will, asserting in the end the delicate balance that we mentioned above. He adds an interesting reflec-
tion about human will:

> God grants to us free will . . . and accepts it as an invitation to His
> Will and Willpower, and promises to establish the most essen-
> tial projects upon this will, a plan He has implemented and
> continues to do so. God created our will as an occasion of merit
> or sin, and as a basis for recompense and punishment, and
> accepts it as an agent for ascribing to good and evil . . . This is
> why God attaches importance to our will and to the desires and
> wishes of humanity; He accepts it as a condition for the con-
> struction and prosperity of both this world and the Hereafter,
> making it a considerable cause, like a magical switch to a pow-
> erful electrical mechanism that can illuminate the worlds.[18]

So, here Gülen asserts that the mechanism of human will,
established by God, is the mechanism that determines the realities
of both this world and the Hereafter. To assert the supreme signif-
icance of human will and action in the world in no way undermines
the will of God; indeed, human will is the confirmation and the
execution of God's will in the world, which is why departure from
humaneness, faith, knowledge, and truth is so very problematic. To
depart from these things is to abdicate the office of responsible

vicegerency and to use the powers of that supreme office for ill, which impacts life at the most profound levels because the domain of accountability for that office includes both the entirety of this world and the next, in short, all reality.

We begin to see, then, the beginning of a tone that Gülen takes throughout *The Statue of Our Souls*, a tone of passion and urgency that calls forth people who will fully take on this title of vicegerent and will bear on their backs the weight of responsibility inherent to the role. Throughout the rest of the book, Gülen details the character traits of these vicegerents, many of which we have already discussed in the previous two chapters, because the ultimate vicegerents are the "inheritors of the earth," the "people of heart," or the "ideal people." Here, however, we focus on those character traits that link directly to responsibility for the world. One of these traits is action, or being a person of action. Gülen explains:

> Action is the most important and necessary component of our lives. By undertaking particular responsibilities through continuous acting and thinking, by facing and bearing particular difficulties, almost in a sense, by sentencing ourselves to all these, even though it may be at the expense of many things, we always have to act, to strive. If we do not act as we are, we are dragged into the waves caused by the thrust and actions of others, and into the whirlpools of the plans and thoughts of others, and then we are forced to act on behalf of others. Remaining aloof from action, not interfering in the things happening around us, nor being a part of the events around us and staying indifferent to them is like letting ourselves melt away, like ice turning to water.[19]

Astute readers will sense already the lines of resonance between Gülen and Sartre on this particular point. Gülen here identifies action as the chief component of human life. Only through action do we become the inheritors of the earth in the way described in earlier chapters. Only through action do we create ourselves and the world in the way discussed in this chapter. Without action, that is, involving ourselves, taking responsibility for things and bearing the suffering that responsibility naturally involves, we relinquish

ourselves to the actions of others, we relinquish our role as humans
and as vicegerents and choose, instead, a pre- or other-determined
life similar to the existence of inanimate objects or animals who live
according to hardwired instinct instead of choice and conscience.
Our human beingness melts away from us when we refuse to act
and to bear the responsibilities of action. In another passage, Gülen
says that in choosing not to act (which of course is an action in
itself, albeit an irresponsible one) we are choosing death: "The most
deeply significant aspect of existence is action and effort. Inertia is
dissolving, decomposition, and another name for death."[20]

Gülen says that people of action take many roles in society,
"sometimes a loyal patriot, a hero of thoughtful action, sometimes
a devoted disciple of science and learning, an artist of genius, a
statesperson, and sometimes all of these."[21] He spends an entire
chapter summarizing the lives and work of recent figures in Turkish
history. What distinguishes and unites them all, according to Gülen,
is the incredible mantle of responsibility they wear for virtually
everything, the call of the Infinite they hear ringing throughout
their conscience that they are responsible for the world and that
every molecule of their being and energy must be in the active service of that charge. Gülen explains:

> Their responsibility is such that whatever enters an individual's
> comprehension and conscious willpower never remains outside
> of theirs: responsibility for the creation and events, nature and
> society, the past and the future, the dead and the living, the
> young and the old, the literate and the illiterate, administration
> and security . . . everybody and everything. And of course they
> feel the pain of all these responsibilities in their heart; they
> make themselves felt as maddening palpitations, exasperation
> in the soul, always competing for their attention . . . The pain
> and distress that arise from the consciousness of responsibility,
> if it is not temporary, is a prayer, a supplication which is not reject-
> ed, and a powerful source of further alternative projects, and
> the note most appealing to consciences which have remained
> clear and uncorrupted.[22]

This is an extraordinary passage. First, notice the domain of responsibility, "everybody and everything," including the past and the dead. Nothing that can come into comprehension or consciousness is outside the domain of this responsibility. If we can think of it and it is real (not imaginary), we are responsible for it. Second, notice the suffering that is the companion of responsibility, the "pain and distress" that comes with this consciousness. Gülen in this passage, and elsewhere in his work, speaks of the inner hardship that comes with taking seriously the role of vicegerent, of inheritor of the earth. Often, he echoes Rumi, the great thirteenth-century poet who writes so eloquently of the pain and suffering that accompanies great love, and of the anguished yearning for the Beloved that is a profound suffering, yet the lover will not give it up to avoid the suffering because the love of the Beloved is the reason for existence, the soul of life itself. Gülen's vicegerents here are lovers of the Beloved, and in this case, the Beloved is God, God's creation, all reality which comes from God, everything and everybody, and to love the Beloved is to be responsible for it. It is a yearning, a suffering, a palpitation of the heart, and a quivering consciousness that is never avoided as long as one is "in love." The lover is sentenced to it as a lover. It is not an obstacle to love. It is the very condition of that love. Finally, the passage above indicates that this responsibility is the homing bell of all true human beings, and that whenever they hear the "note" of this bell through the suffering, they activate more projects and plans. Gülen says people of responsibility love this responsibility so much that they would even give up Paradise for it.[23]

The resonance with Sartre is obvious even as we acknowledge that Gülen and Sartre generate their ideas and work from within utterly different philosophical frames, so much so that it seems unlikely at first glance that there should exist any resonance whatsoever between them. What is clear, however, is that each of them from their respective and vastly different starting points, and within divergent worldviews, articulate parallel views of human life in the world with regard to human responsibility for the world. Both

Sartre and Gülen give their complete intellectual energies to high-lighting the urgent need in life for people to take responsibility for the world, and to reiterating the fact that the world has always been and will continue to be that which we make of it. Thus it is that either man, Gülen or Sartre, could have written these words from *The Statue of Our Souls*:

> Each and every person who has a sense of serious individual responsibility will say "I have to do this myself. If I do not do it now, to whatever extent I can, then probably no one will do it," and they will run forward to be the first to do it, to bear the flag high.[24]

We must rely on ourselves and our own powers, regardless of whether we believe they come to us from God, as Gülen does, or not, like Sartre, and refuse to expect something or someone outside of us to do our work for us. To push our responsibility onto others is to live in "bad faith," to use Sartre's phrase which, interestingly, squares quite well with Gülen's assessment of people of faith who refuse responsibility—they live a "bad faith."

A final quote from Gülen seals his vision for true human life and flourishing and illumines exactly what must take place if a world of goodness, truth, and freedom for everyone is to come into being and the role that people play in bringing that world into being. Again, the spirit of the quote resonates with the spirit, albeit not the letter, of Sartrean sensibilities. Gülen says:

> In fact, we need genius minds with iron wills that are able to carry the title of vicegerent of God on Earth, and which are able to intervene in events and challenge the orphan spirit and puny thought which attach no importance to the consciousness of responsibility, humane values, knowledge, morality, true contemplation, virtue, and art in such a vast territory, we need refined minds and an iron will which will embrace and interpret creation in its depth and entirety and humanity in all its worldly and other-worldly vastness.[25]

The deep spirit here is bravery, the bravery of responsibility. In our cowardice and bad faith, we flee from responsibility for our own lives and for the world. We, from a cowardly and puny spirit, make excuses for ourselves and blame the world situation on others, or on fate, or on circumstances. All the while, the world rests on our shoulders, whether or not we acknowledge it, or take on the charge of that accountability. The world still rests on our shoulders even as we choose death and inertia, the life of a piece of moss, or a chair, or rock, the life less than that which is designed for us by God, or Nature, or Existence. Authentic life, in the eyes of God, or in the eyes of Life, is the life of accountability, and those who live it suffer the despair and anguish of that life, but they are also the beings who truly deserve the designation "human." They have iron wills and brave hearts that push them forward amidst their distress into ever expanded domains of responsibility for everyone and everything. These individuals are the true heroes of humanity, and it is on their backs that the world is made. As both Gülen and Sartre affirm, human society always has been, and will continue to be, what we human beings make of it.

CONCLUSION

During the writing of this book, I had the very special opportunity to meet Mr. Gülen and to share two meals with him at the retreat center where he lives. He was very gracious to us and spent considerable time with us, despite being quite ill. He answered some of my questions, and those who were present discussed the issues of the day with him and eagerly received his insights. Of course, I have "lived" with Gülen in textual form during the writing of this book. I remain inspired by his ideas, and after meeting him I see why he has inspired nearly three generations now of Turkish men and women to create a new world. He is a man of deep spirituality, integrity, and compassion, and this is amply evident in his writings and in his person.

I have partnered Gülen's ideas with those of Kant, Plato, Confucius, Mill, and Sartre because I believe they are worthy discussants for Gülen, and he for them. I interpret all of them as people with immense knowledge who care about the most pressing and enduring questions of human existence, and who approach difficult challenges with their whole selves honestly and without cynicism. They are fine representatives of the best kind of scholarship in the humanities, the kind that provides sophisticated analysis in order to apply it to the world and our life in it, so that we may learn what comprises the good life and achieve it for ourselves and for future generations. Scholarship that does not have this as its ultimate goal is not authentic scholarship.

I am inspired by the engagement of ideas I have enacted here. I am not inspired because I agree totally with any one perspective presented here. Rather, I am inspired by the conversation itself and the possibilities that such conversations offer when conducted not only in the pages of a book but in real life with living participants.

I know that I have stretched terms, themes, and passages quite thin in attempting to establish resonance between the discussants. I know that, in many instances, that resonance will hold, if at all, for only so long before the thread of connection snaps due to its thinness and the weight of difference pulling it from both sides. If the connection is enough to hold just for a little while, however, relatedness is achieved at least for those few moments. In the pages of texts, and with discussants long dead, relatedness happens only in the abstract. With live participants, those of us willing to engage, interact, and who are, in fact, responsible for the world and everyone and everything, the relatedness established in those moments of stretch is not abstract; it is real. Perhaps, that relatedness can then prevent us from demonizing and killing each other, symbolically and literally, after the thin thread breaks, and we become yet again confronted by our radical difference.

Developing strategies and capacities for peaceful co-existence amidst radical difference and shrinking natural resources is the central challenge of our era. We must give our best selves to this challenge, or all our other achievements will fail because we will have exploded the world with our hatred and violence. May we find within us, as human beings called by the Infinite in all its modes, the character to transcend ourselves and to create a world of tolerance, respect, and compassion.

NOTES

INTRODUCTION

1 For more on humanism, its various subdivisions, and its interface with religion and Islam, see: Guthrie 1969; Rabil, Jr. 1988; Davidson 1992; Fakhry 1983; Goodman 2003; Kraye 1996.

CHAPTER 1
Gülen and Kant on Inherent Human Value and Moral Dignity

1 Kant, *Grounding for the Metaphysics of Morals*, 5.

2 Ibid., 7.

3 Ibid., 8.

4 Ibid., 9.

5 Ibid.

6 Ibid., 14.

7 Ibid., 36.

8 Ibid.

9 Ibid., 40–1.

10 Ibid., 41.

11 Ibid., 42.

12 Ibid., 43.

13 Gülen, *Toward a Global Civilization of Love and Tolerance*, 112.

14 Ibid.

15 Ibid., 113.

16 Ibid., 116.

17 Ibid., 169.

18 Ibid., 114.

19 Ibid., 8.

20 Ibid., 8–9.

21 Ibid., 221.

22 Ibid., 224.

CHAPTER 2
Gülen and Mill on Freedom

[1]　Mill, *On Liberty*, 41.
[2]　Ibid., 44.
[3]　Ibid., 48.
[4]　Ibid., 67.
[5]　Ibid.
[6]　Ibid.
[7]　Gülen, *Pearls of Wisdom*, 55.
[8]　Gülen, *Toward a Global Civilization of Love and Tolerance*, 44.
[9]　Gülen, *The Statue of Our Souls*, 5–10, 31–42.
[10]　Ibid., 38.
[11]　Ibid., 38–9.
[12]　Ibid., 39.
[13]　Ibid., 40.
[14]　Mill, *Utilitarianism*, 7.
[15]　Ibid.
[16]　Ibid., 8.
[17]　Ibid., 9.
[18]　Ibid., 10.
[19]　Gülen, *Pearls of Wisdom*, 55.

CHAPTER 3
Gülen, Confucius, and Plato on the Human Ideal

[1]　Confucius, *The Analects*, 146.
[2]　Ibid., 132.
[3]　Ibid., 176.
[4]　Ibid., 188–9.
[5]　Ibid., 189.
[6]　Plato, *The Republic*, 277–8.
[7]　Ibid., 209–11.
[8]　Ibid., 212.
[9]　Gülen, *The Statue of Our Souls*, 5ff.
[10]　Ibid., 125–6.
[11]　Gülen, *Toward a Global Civilization of Love and Tolerance*, 128–30.
[12]　Gülen, *The Statue of Our Souls*, 135.
[13]　Ibid., 135–6.

14 Gülen, *Toward a Global Civilization of Love and Tolerance*, 113.
15 Thompson, *Chinese Religion*, 13.
16 Confucius, *The Analects*, 127.
17 Ibid., 11.
18 Ibid.
19 Ibid.
20 Ibid., 95.
21 Plato, *The Republic*, 41.
22 Ibid., 165.
23 Gülen, *The Statue of Our Souls*, 124.
24 Ibid.
25 Ibid., 119.
26 Ibid., 5.
27 Ibid.
28 Ibid., 31–42.
29 Ibid., 89.
30 Gülen, *Pearls of Wisdom*, 71–2.
31 Ibid., 73.
32 Gülen, *Toward a Global Civilization of Love and Tolerance*, 82.

CHAPTER 4
Gülen, Confucius, and Plato on Education

1 Confucius, *The Analects*, xxiv–xxv.
2 Ibid., 198.
3 Ibid., 178.
4 Thompson, *Chinese Religion*, 145–6.
5 Confucius, *The Analects*, 198.
6 Ibid., 199.
7 Plato, *The Republic*, 113–4.
8 Ibid., 109.
9 Ibid., 73.
10 Ibid., 99.
11 Ibid.
12 Ibid., 137.
13 Gülen, *Essays, Perspectives, Opinions*, 80.
14 Gülen, *Pearls of Wisdom*, 231–2.
15 Gülen, *Toward a Global Civilization of Love and Tolerance*, 202.
16 Ibid., 217.

[17] Ibid., 206–7.

[18] Gülen, *The Statue of Our Souls*, 45.

[19] Ibid., 54–5.

[20] Ibid., 55.

CHAPTER 5

Gülen and Sartre on Responsibility

[1] Gülen, *The Statue of Our Souls*, 35.

[2] Sartre, "Existentialism" in *Basic Writings of Existentialism*, 345.

[3] Ibid., 346–7.

[4] Ibid.

[5] Ibid., 358.

[6] Ibid., 348.

[7] Ibid., 347.

[8] Ibid., 348.

[9] Ibid., 349.

[10] Ibid.

[11] Ibid., 367.

[12] Ibid., 354.

[13] Ibid., 355.

[14] Ibid., 357.

[15] Gülen, *Toward a Global Civilization of Love and Tolerance*, 122.

[16] Ibid.

[17] Ibid., 124–5.

[18] Gülen, *The Statue of Our Souls*, 15.

[19] Ibid., 59.

[20] Ibid., 99.

[21] Ibid., 68.

[22] Ibid., 95.

[23] Ibid., 97.

[24] Ibid., 154.

[25] Ibid., 105.

BIBLIOGRAPHY

Confucius. *The Analects*. Trans. David Hinton. Washington, D.C.: Counterpoint, 1998.

Davidson, Herbert A. *Alfarabi, Avicenna, and Averroes on Intellect*. Oxford: Oxford University Press, 1992.

Fakhry, Majid. *A History of Islamic Philosophy*. New York: Columbia University Press, 1983. (First edition 1970)

Goodman, Lenn E. *Islamic Humanism*. Oxford: Oxford University Press, 2003.

Gülen, M. Fethullah. *Pearls of Wisdom*. Fairfax: The Fountain, 2000.

——. *Toward a Global Civilization of Love and Tolerance*. New Jersey: The Light Inc., 2004.

——. *The Statue of Our Souls: Revival in Islamic Thought and Activism*. New Jersey: The Light Inc., 2005.

——. *Essays, Perspectives, Opinions*. New Jersey: The Light Inc., 2005.

Guthrie, W.K.C. *A History of Greek Philosophy*. Cambridge: Cambridge University Press, 1969.

Kant, Immanuel. *Grounding for the Metaphysics of Morals*. Third edition. Trans. James W. Ellington. Indianapolis: Hackett Publishing Company, 1993.

Kraye, Jill, ed. *The Cambridge Companion to Renaissance Humanism*. Cambridge: Cambridge University Press, 1996.

Mill, John Stuart. *On Liberty*, A Norton Critical Edition. Ed. Alan Ryan. New York: W. W. Norton, 1997.

——. *Utilitarianism*. Indianapolis: Hackett Publishing Company, 1979.

Plato. *The Republic*. Trans. Richard W. Sterling and William C. Scott. New York: W. W. Norton, 1985.

Rabil Jr., Albert, ed. *Renaissance Humanism: Foundation, Forms and Legacy*. 3 vols. Philadelphia: Pennsylvania University Press, 1988.

Sartre, Jean Paul. "Existentialism" in *Basic Writings of Existentialism*. Ed. Gordon Marino. New York: The Modern Library, 2004.

Thompson, Laurence G. *Chinese Religion: An Introduction*. Fifth edition. Belmont, CA: Wadsworth Publishing Company, 1996.

INDEX